COCKS AND HENS

Ian Taylor

BROADWAY PLAY PUBLISHING INC
New York
www.broadwayplaypublishing.com
info@broadwayplaypublishing.com

COCKS AND HENS
© Copyright 1975, 1985 Ian Taylor

All rights reserved. This work is fully protected under the copyright laws of the United States of America. No part of this publication may be photocopied, reproduced, stored in a retrieval system, or transmitted, in any form or by any means, electronic, mechanical, recording, or otherwise, without the prior permission of the publisher. Additional copies of this play are available from the publisher.

Written permission is required for live performance of any sort. This includes readings, cuttings, scenes, and excerpts. For amateur and stock performances, please contact Broadway Play Publishing Inc. For all other rights please contact Valerie Hoskins Associates, 20 Charlotte St, London, W1T 2NA, 020 7637 4490, info@vhassociates.co.uk..

Cover art by Craig Nealy

First edition: September 1986
This edition: October 2017
I S B N: 978-0-88145-034-7

Book design: Marie Donovan
Typefaces: Palatino & Aster by Techna-Type, Inc, York, PA

Characters

ANGELA
JUDITH
BAILEY
JACKO
JEFF

Note on setting: The stage is split into two areas—

    The Office Area—known as Stage One
    The River Bank—known as Stage Two

In the final scene in the play the whole stage may be used in full. Both stages become one: The Office.

The settings should be simple and sparse—they should contain as little as possible, be just impressionistic.

ACT ONE

Scene One

(*Lights up on Stage One: An improvised office in an old house by a river. Early on a summer's afternoon. There is an atmosphere in the office of heat and boredom.*)

(JUDITH *is reading figures from invoices for* ANGELA *to put into a calculator.*)

(ANGELA, *after sniffling, coughing, wiping her nose on a Kleenex tissue, says, tiredly:*)

ANGELA: Got that. Carry on.

JUDITH: Twenty-five pounds twenty.

ANGELA: Yes.

JUDITH: Thirty pounds twenty-one.

ANGELA: Ye'.

JUDITH: Seventy pounds thirteen.

ANGELA: Right.

JUDITH: Clickety click pounds clickety.

ANGELA: Uh? Oh, ah, right.

JUDITH: Sorry. Just trying to make things more interesting.

ANGELA: Nearly threw me out, you . . .

JUDITH: Six er steener six.

ANGELA: Sex er steener sex. Righ'.

JUDITH: (*Livening herself up; fearing descent into silliness.*) Thirty-two pounds two.

ANGELA: (*Briskly*) Okay.

JUDITH: Twenty pounds only.

ANGELA: (*Briskly*) Okay.

JUDITH: Thirty pounds thirty.

ANGELA: Okay.

JUDITH: Sixty-four pounds fourteen.

ANGELA: O—kay.

JUDITH: (*Sharply*) Three pounds.

ANGELA: Uh?

JUDITH: (*Sharply*) Three pounds.

ANGELA: Three pounds. Right.

JUDITH: Three pounds . . .

ANGELA: Right.

JUDITH: Fourteen.

ANGELA: Wha'?

JUDITH: Three pounds fourteen.

ANGELA: Bugger! (*She readjusts figures in machine.*) Right. Stop mucking about, you bugger. What was it again . . . ? Just a minid . . . (*She sneezes loudly—doesn't use Kleenex.*) Ride what wad it?

JUDITH: Three pounds fourteen pence.

ANGELA: Three pounds fourteen pence.

JUDITH: Correct.

ANGELA: Carry on.

JUDITH: Two pounds only.

ANGELA: Do pounds only. Yep.

JUDITH: Sixty-nine pounds three . . .

ANGELA: Just a minid. (*She blows her nose; throws Kleenex tissue toward basket.* JUDITH *looks at her and at tissue but refrains from comment.*)

ANGELA: The pollen, this time of the year, always get me . . .

JUDITH: It's the middle of summer!

ANGELA: Don't matter always gets me. Right down into the sinuses. You have that problem?

ACT ONE

JUDITH: I should think the smell from the works over there would clean anybody's sinuses out. Putrid.

ANGELA: That's better. It's clearing now. Yes. That's good, I can breathe. Now where were we?

JUDITH: Sixty-nine pounds three.

ANGELA: Right.

JUDITH: Ten pounds.

ANGELA: Ten pounds.

JUDITH: And thirteen pounds ten . . .

ANGELA: Right.

(*She waits.* JUDITH *gives room a quick spray of air freshener.* ANGELA *coughs.*)

JUDITH: Sorry. It's a health hazard in here.

ANGELA: Ye' it is.

JUDITH: Like the Black Hole of Calcutta.

ANGELA: (*Indicating adding machine*) How're we fixed now?

(*She taps her fingers while* JUDITH, *having put can of air freshener back in drawer, uses hand lotion.*)

JUDITH: That's it.

ANGELA: All done?

JUDITH: On that batch.

ANGELA: Thank God for that.

JUDITH: What'sit come to?

(ANGELA *uses calculator.*)

ANGELA: (*After a moment*) Four thousand, six hundred and ninety-five pounds and forty-nine pence.

JUDITH: (*Mock exuberance*) Hurray!

ANGELA: Does it tally?

JUDITH: Do you want to check back?

ANGELA: Na, it'll be all right.

JUDITH: Sure?

ANGELA: Ye' course.

(*She passes across adding machine list for* JUDITH *to pin to batch of invoices. She uses* JUDITH'*s hand lotion.*)

(JUDITH *efficiently ties up bundle of invoices to lay down on another pile.* ANGELA *stands up, looks around office, peeved. At the other batches of invoices:*)

ANGELA: Gawd'strewth! How long do you reckon it'll take us to finish this lot?

JUDITH: Years.

ANGELA: Bloody stroll on.

JUDITH: I suppose if we really got into it we could get rid of it by tonight.

(ANGELA *flaps front of her blouse, fans herself with a loose invoice. Bothered by the heat, goes over to window.*)

ANGELA: (*At window*) Bloody stroll on. I've never known such a boring blimmin' job in all my life. That's the trouble with being a temp, you always get the most boring jobs. Good job it's only for a couple of weeks. Drive me bananas else.

(ANGELA *wipes nose on back of her hand. She puts on sun glasses, remains at window looking out, at first indolently.*)

ANGELA: And look at that lovely, lovely sunshine out there, all shining along the river. Them lovely little ducks under the bushes. Nice 'en it, eh? It's so lovely and warm. Christ, I wish I'd brought me cossy. Coulda worked up a bit of a tan here through this window. If I'd known there'd only be the two of us up here I would have done.

JUDITH: Don't mind me.

ANGELA: Eh?

JUDITH: Strip down to the very buff if you wish.

ANGELA: Eh?

JUDITH: Be my guest.

ACT ONE

ANGELA: (*After some thought*) No thanks I'll wait 'til I know you better.

JUDITH: No need to worry about me.

ANGELA: Never know these days.

(JUDITH *laughs, shakes her head at* ANGELA's *tone of voice in what she says. She finds another batch of invoices to be added, goes across to table.*)

JUDITH: Ready for another session?

ANGELA: Wha' . . . Oh, Ah, I s'pose so . . .

JUDITH: Once more into the breach, dear friends . . .

ANGELA: Once more into the breach is right. Like bein' on a bleedn' tread mill . . .

JUDITH: Perhaps if we'd made the right kind of noises we'd have had some help sent out here.

ANGELA: Not this firm, mate. Notorious. Slave labor, that's all we are.

JUDITH: All the same I'd have thought there should have been more than two of us out here.

ANGELA: You take too much notice of all those jolly-with-it adverts at the agency.

JUDITH: No, I know better than that.

ANGELA: Where they have film cameras in the window, as if you're signing on to make a epic instead of. . . . He . . . y . . . well . . .

JUDITH: I just thought this is a bit of a lonely spot . . . and . . .

(*She looks up to find that* ANGELA *seems to have lost all interest in the conversation and is looking at something that is going on below, in the distance, across the river. At the same time* (*Off*), *a clarion or buzzer sounds from the works across the river.*)

(JUDITH *continues putting invoices into alphabetical and then company order: a laborious job. Now and again she looks over at* ANGELA *to see if she will eventually come and help her. But*

ANGELA *remains at window, not interested in what* JUDITH *is doing. She is more interested in what is going on across the river. Her interest becomes even more intensified.*)

ANGELA: Mmmmmmmmmmm. Mmmmmmmmmm. Ymmmmmmmm. Yes, well now, what have we here . . . ?

(JUDITH *looks around once or twice, irritated by* ANGELA's *apparent laziness, but does not say anything.*)

ANGELA: (*To herself*) Now, I know him. Ye', I know him. Seen him around. Used to have a motor-bike. Crashed it. Ye'. I like his trilby an er . . . he's er . . . a bit . . . er . . . but dunno if I like him much . . . I 'spect he could er . . . But . . . Hmmmm . . . I could quite fancy that little one. Yes, he's er, okay. Could quite fancy . . . Don't like him though. That big ugly . . .

JUDITH: Who're you looking at?

ANGELA: These down here.

JUDITH: Oh. I see.

ANGELA: They've just come out of the works across the river. That engineering place. Must be going down the river bank for their lunch. Yes. They are.

(JUDITH *continues working.* ANGELA *remains at window, though taking care at this stage not to put herself in full view.*)

(*This position:* JUDITH *working,* ANGELA, *looking out, remains for as long as possible.*)

JUDITH: (*Finally irritated. Sharply.*) Come on, then?

ANGELA: Eh?

JUDITH: Aren't you going to give me some help?

ANGELA: Come over here.

JUDITH: We do want to get finished don't we?

ANGELA: Uh? Oh. It's too hot . . . (*She continues looking down.*)

ACT ONE

JUDITH: Angela!

ANGELA: Hang about. Hey . . . He . . . y ye . . . yey . . . Wow . . .

(ANGELA *lifts her sunglasses, suddenly begins to look very interested indeed, and very astonished. At least she affects astonishment.*)

ANGELA: Cheeky bugger! . . . Judith!

JUDITH: What?

ANGELA: Cheeky buggers. (*Hurriedly signalling*) Judith! Comeanavealook. Quick. Come on . . . hurry . . .

JUDITH: Oh . . . all right . . .

(ANGELA *signals to* JUDITH *to keep out of sight and remain quiet. Judith tiptoes across the office and stands behind* ANGELA.)

(ANGELA, *grinning, points downwards.* JUDITH *raises herself on tiptoe to look over* ANGELA's *shoulder to where she is pointing.*)

ANGELA: These two (*She whispers*). They're having a pee.

JUDITH: Oh! Oh! Well. . . .

ANGELA: (*Beginning to giggle*) Stood there. Bold as brass.

JUDITH: Oh, my . . . Like a couple of Lords . . .

ANGELA: Jeezus, will you look at that one. That big old bloke, I mean he's gorra . . .

JUDITH: Bit to be proud of . . .

ANGELA: Jeeze . . . Have you ever seen the . . . Jeeze . . .

JUDITH: Yes, it's er. . . .

ANGELA: Struth! They don't care, do they?

JUDITH: They don't know they're under observation . . .

ANGELA: Struth. My fiancé hasn't got . . . I mean . . . anything like . . .

JUDITH: Now look what they're doing . . .

ANGELA: Ah, ha . . . So that's what they do . . .

(*The two women stand still, watching.*)

(*BLACKOUT STAGE ONE*)

Scene Two

(*Lights up on Stage Two.*)

(*A piece of rough ground, waste ground, by the river, on the opposite side to the house where* JUDITH *and* ANGELA *are working.*)

(*This area is in full sunlight. One of those hot, still sort of days, broken only now and then by sound of a waterfowl, frog croaks, etc.*)

(*Perhaps a piece of driftwood or an old log are around, or packing boxes, etc.*)

(*As lights come up,* JEFF *is selecting a spot to sit and read, and is just about to pull a paperback from his back pocket.*)

(BAILEY *and* JACKO, *down front of stage (i.e., on edge of river bank), are just in the act of zipping up.*)

BAILEY: Mine was highest.

JACKO: Rubbish!

BAILEY: (*Legs straddled: mucho hombre*) The advantage I had?

JACKO: (*Struggling, tilting trilby (soft felt hat) over his eyes. Scratching himself through his t-shirt.*) Ya' well . . .

BAILEY: When you're talking about weaponry.

JACKO: We don't include you, Bailey.

BAILEY: (*Chuckling, pleased at* JACKO's *admission.*) Yeah, I'm in a class of my own.

JACKO: (*Angling a sly look around at* JEFF, *to rope him in as an accomplice.*) I'd rather lie under a fall of stone.

BAILEY: You wha'?

ACT ONE 9

JACKO: Said that's right—you're in a class of your own. (*With a wink aside to* JEFF.) The Ape class!

BAILEY: You have to admit the equipment is superior.

JACKO: Bloody unnatural. (*He's about to grin around at* JEFF, *but* BAILEY *catches him. He smiles at* BAILEY *instead, tips his hat as if in compliment.*)

BAILEY: Oh, it's natural all right.

JACKO: Yeah, I know.

BAILEY: Not unnaturally raised.

JACKO: Not you, Bailey.

BAILEY: Not hand raised.

(*He winks at* JACKO. *Indicates* JEFF, *who is just settling down with his book. They both watch* JEFF.)

BAILEY: Not hand cranked.

(BAILEY *makes lewd gesture, smacking back of his own neck with the palm of his hand, whilst showing a fist and muscle-bulged forearm.* JACKO, *laughing, picks up flagon of ale.*)

BAILEY: My name ain't J. Arthur. . . .

BAILEY: I believe in natural growth.

JACKO: (*About to put flagon of ale to his lips: snickering down at* JEFF, *with* BAILEY *looming over him, breathing down his neck, waiting for his turn with the ale.*) Not like one of our number.

BAILEY: Natural exercise is the way for growth. All mine was natural exercise. Having fathered many at home and away. Some I do not know about. But I look around this town and I see many coming along who have my stamp on 'em.

(JACKO—*snickering. Big man. Trying to match* BAILEY. *He wipes his lips, about to pass flagon across to* BAILEY. BAILEY, *with a contemptuous gesture, takes it from him.*)

JACKO: Yeah, natural growth is the way all right.

(JACKO *nudges* JEFF *with his foot.* JEFF *looks up and smiles very sweetly.*)

JEFF: Okay, Jacko?

JACKO: Here—this free advice you're getting?

JEFF: Who could fail?

JACKO: Eh?

JEFF: You've repeated the same line over and over again.

JACKO: Well, you just listen and take it in.

JEFF: Okay.

JACKO: Eh?

JEFF: (*Smiling, nodding rapidly, like a puppet, a ventriloquist's dummy.*) Ye'. Ye'. Okay. I'm listenin', I'm listenin'.

JACKO: You never know when such advice is gonna come in handy.

JEFF: You're right, Jacko.

BAILEY: (*Belching*) Seems to me he's handy enough.

(JACKO *laughs.* BAILEY *laughs at his own witticism.*)

JACKO: Hear that, Jeff?

JEFF: I heard.

BAILEY: (*Milking his gag*) He's a pretty handy guy. But he's handy in the wrong way.

(JACKO *titters and remains smiling down on* JEFF.)

JACKO: But I don't reckon there'll be enough there to begin raising by hand even.

(JACKO *smiles, touches* JEFF *with his foot again.*)

JACKO: That right, Jeff?

JEFF: (*Smiling sweetly*) Right, Jacko.

JACKO: Eh, Jeff?

JEFF: If that's what you want to believe, Jacko.

JACKO: (*Mimicking* JEFF's *accent almost perfectly, a surprising skill.*) If that's what you want to believe, Jacko . . . Prick.

ACT ONE

(*To* BAILEY) You can tell he went to Borstal, the way he talks so posh.

(*Borstal, a gag—he thinks* JEFF *went to a good public school because he speaks well, or more gently than he.*)

JEFF: Anything you say, Jacko.

JACKO: Tch.

(JEFF *switches off* JACKO, *reads his book.* JACKO *continues to watch him.*)

JACKO: There you are, reading your books. Always reading your books.

BAILEY: (*Smacking his lips after ale.*) Wants it real. Not in books.

JACKO: Can't take it real. Sooner have it in books, eh, Jeff?

BAILEY: Not in books.

JACKO: You listenin', Jeff?

BAILEY: Load o' bollocks.

JACKO: Books.

BAILEY: Get it real.

JACKO: D'you hear?

JEFF: (*Becoming annoyed at the attention.*) Yes, I expect you're right.

JACKO: It's right. (BAILEY *passes him the flagon.* JACKO *has long pull, passes it back to* BAILEY, *looks down on* JEFF *again.*) Too right, it's right.

BAILEY: He'd never get anywhere near it though, would he?

JACKO: (*After thinking a few moments*) Naw, don't reckon he got enough to interest anybody. What d'you think, Bailey?

BAILEY: Never lets you have a look at it to pass proper judgment.

JACKO: You've seen his old nudger, haven't you?

BAILEY: No.

JACKO: Haven't you?

BAILEY: He always sneaks off when he takes a leak, or keeps his hand over it.

JACKO: (*Matter of fact*) Come on Jeff.

(*No answer.*)

JACKO: Now then Jeff.

(*No answer.*)

JACKO: Jeff. Jeff, what is this?

JEFF: Leave off, Jacko.

JACKO: (*Seriously*) Come on, for Chrissakes.

BAILEY: Yeah.

JACKO: Let Bailey have a see.

JEFF: (*Cool*) Forget it.

JACKO: Come on.

BAILEY: Now Jeff.

JACKO: Just nip it out.

BAILEY: See what you're made of.

JACKO: Let Doctor Bailey advise you on it.

BAILEY: Right.

JACKO: (*Moving in on* JEFF.) Come on Jeff.

JEFF: Piss off.

JACKO: Language! Not right, such language! In one so young.

(JEFF *puts out his feet, keeps* JACKO *off.* JACKO *circles.*)

JACKO: I'll get you.

JEFF: Go 'way.

JACKO: Jacko's goin't to get you. Oh, yes he is. Gotcha!

JEFF: Ow!

ACT ONE

(JACKO *gets* JEFF *in a Japanese leglock.*)

JEFF: (*Helpless*) Ow, you bastard!

JACKO: Ain't no bastard, boy.

JEFF: Bastard.

JACKO: Just bein' cruel to be kind.

JEFF: Rotten bastard.

(JACKO *tightens the grip.*)

JACKO: Now, nip it out like a good little boy. Out wit yer little ding dong den Doctor Bailey can examin yer. Come on.

(BAILEY, *with flagon of ale, guffaws at* JACKO's *nonsense.*)

JACKO: Get his fly, Bailey.

JEFF: Bailey!

(BAILEY *looks as if he might go over to* JEFF, *then stays where he is.*)

JACKO: See the hold I got on him.

BAILEY: You can get out of that can't you, Jeff?

JACKO: Never.

JEFF: Bastard.

JACKO: Gerris cock, Bailey.

JEFF: No . . . You bloody won't.

(*With a great effort he twists his ankle from under* JACKO's *foot, puts* JACKO *off balance so that by rolling over on his stomach he twists his foot from under* JACKO's *armpit and sends* JACKO *sprawling.* BAILEY, *noting* JEFF's *surprising piece of wrestling skill, nods approvingly.*)

BAILEY: Well done, kid.

JACKO: Yer little gett.

(*He jumps on* JEFF's *back and pulls at* JEFF's *trousers.*)

JACKO: Come on yer little prick.

JEFF: Get off me, you shite.

(JACKO *lies on top of* JEFF *and works his hands under* JEFF, *feeling around his privates, licking at* JEFF's *ear seductively.*)

JACKO: Come on darlin', what's the matter with yer? Eh, come on. What's afraid of? Nobody's goin' to hurt you.

BAILEY: (*With flagon again, laughing at* JACKO.) Bloody fool, Jacko.

JACKO: Come on, Jeff, wassermarrer, den?

JEFF: There's a couple of chicks up there watching all this.

JACKO: (*Turning*) Where?

JEFF: Over the river.

(JEFF *points around* JACKO. JACKO *gets up off* JEFF. BAILEY *turns to look across river.*)

BAILEY: Where?

JEFF: That old house across the river?

JACKO: Yeah?

JEFF: That window that's open? Upstairs. Second floor.

BAILEY and JACKO: (*Nodding*) Yeah?

JEFF: In there.

BAILEY and JACKO: Go on!

JEFF: A couple o' chicks are hiding behind the shutters. If you keep looking you'll see them.

(BAILEY *and* JACKO *stand closer to the edge of stage* (*river bank*). *They shield their eyes from the sun.* JEFF *starts to straighten his clothing, dust himself off.*)

BAILEY: It's empty that place, isn't it?

JACKO: I never seen anybody in there.

BAILEY: Nor me.

JACKO: Empty.

BAILEY: Always been empty as long as I've worked

ACT ONE

back there. Nobody there all last summer. I know that. Creepy flippin' place. Looks haunted to me.

JACKO: Yeah, definitely creepy.

(JEFF *has picked up his book and looks as if he may take off.* JACKO *sees him.*)

JACKO: Hey, Jeffo, what is this?

JEFF: Told you. They were watching you having a slash.

BAILEY: (*Swinging aroung to look at* JEFF, *almost as if he's embarrassed by the idea.*) Ya?

JEFF: (*Scoring*) Yes.

BAILEY: What when we were . . .

JEFF: They were laughing at you.

BAILEY: Laughin'?

JACKO: Laughin' at us? No bird's laughing at my dickie and gettin' away with it.

BAILEY: You wouldn't chuckle.

(JACKO *and* BAILEY *stare again at the house.*)

JACKO: (*Muttering*) No bird's laughing at my cock and getting away with it.

BAILEY: Too right. How can we get across there . . . ?

JACKO: Too far to the bridge. Jesus, this gives you something to think about. Birds laughing at your. . . .

(JEFF, *about to slope away again with his book, is grinning. Out of the corner of his eyes,* JACKO *is aware of* JEFF.)

JACKO: Hey!

JEFF: What?

JACKO: Lying gett.

(JACKO *nudges* BAILEY, *indicates* JEFF. *They both look at* JEFF.)

BAILEY: (*With a slight chuckle*) Lying gett, Jeff?

JEFF: Not codding you.

JACKO: (*Moving quickly, heading* JEFF *off*) Lying sod.

JEFF: No. Straight up.

BAILEY: Lying sod, Jeff.

(JACKO *and* BAILEY, *on either side of* JEFF, *grinning in acknowledgment of* JEFF's *nerve.*)

JEFF: Told you.

JACKO: Throw him in the fucking river.

(JEFF *tries to make a break for it.* JACKO *tackles him again and brings him down, hard.* BAILEY *laughing looks on.*)

JACKO: Get hold of him, Bailey. Get his feet.

JEFF: Get off. Not again. Get off.

BAILEY: You asked for it, Jeff.

(BAILEY *grabs* JEFF's *feet.* BAILEY *and* JACKO *lift* JEFF *and carry him to edge of stage as if to throw him in the water.*)

JACKO: In the fucking water with him.

(JEFF *protests as they begin to swing him out over the stage.*)

BAILEY: Ready . . . On a count of three . . .

JACKO: A one a two a . . .

BAILEY: Three . . .

JACKO: In yer go. Inigo.

(*He is held ready to be dropped.*)

BAILEY: Nah, better not. He'll need an injection if we drop him in there. Full of all kind of shit and disease.

JACKO: Deserves it the bugger. Come on, throw him in.

BAILEY: Knew a feller got galloping knob rot from falling in there.

JACKO: Knob fell off?

BAILEY: Right off.

JACKO: Well, it's no good to Jeff: in with him.

ACT ONE

BAILEY: Nah, let him be.

(JEFF *is finally carried back to where he was sitting reading his book, and dumped.*)

BAILEY: You stay there and read your book like a good boy.

JEFF: Yes, Dad.

(BAILEY *gives* JEFF *a pat on the head. Having joked enough, turns away to pick up beer flagon.* JACKO, *who doesn't know when enough is enough, jumps on* JEFF *again, making a final effort to undo his zip.* JEFF *automatically flings out an arm to defend himself and smacks* JACKO *very heavily at the side of the head, very nearly putting* JACKO *down.* BAILEY *laughs. It was an accident.* JEFF *is instantly apologetic.* JACKO *sways, holding his head, rubbing his temple. When he looks at* JEFF *again it is with some real respect. But* BAILEY's *chuckling makes him raw. He tries to cover his feelings with a flip remark.*)

JACKO: She doesn't like her thingie tampered with does she?

JEFF: (*Shrugs. Dismissing* JACKO.) Sorry, Jacko. Accident.

(*But* JACKO *is standing over him again. Menacing, watching like a cat, a hurt cat, not joking, ready to strike, when he can choose his moment. Trying to psyche* JEFF. JEFF *watches* JACKO, *a hand held up, watching, waiting for* JACKO *to strike. They hold like this a moment until* BAILEY *looks across, sees what's happening, and shouts, maybe throwing a piece of scuffling between them.* (*Scuffling: dirt, stones*))

BAILEY: Hey! You two! Leave it now! That's enough. Gone far enough. Christ, day like this and scrapping . . . Come on . . . Jacko. You got your cards on you?

(JACKO *rearranges his trilby, dusts off his t-shirt, and whilst giving* JEFF *a long puzzled look—he can't understand why he can't get the better of* JEFF—*he slowly puts his hand down toward the back pocket of his jeans. He points at* JEFF *with the other hand.*)

JACKO: Anytime, I'm ready for lumber.

(JEFF *opens his book. Shuts* JACKO *out.* BAILEY *reaches over and takes cards from* JACKO's *hand which is just emerging from back pocket of his jeans.*)

JACKO: Just remember. Anytime.

(JEFF *still does not answer.* JACKO *becomes bolder.*)

JACKO: If you ever do that again, I'll do you. Right?

(JEFF *thinks about this and then says quietly:*)

JEFF: Okay, Jacko.

JACKO: Right.

JEFF: If you think you can . . .

(JACKO *is again about to go for* JEFF. BAILEY *reaches out his hand, grabs* JACKO *by the belt, the back of his trousers.*)

BAILEY: Leave him. I said.

JACKO: Little cunt.

BAILEY: Let's play cards. I said let's play cards.

(*He turns* JACKO *away from* JEFF, *indicates to* JEFF *to stay cool, not worry.*)

BAILEY: Siddown, Jacko.

(*They sit cross legged opposite each other,* BAILEY *and* JACKO, *using top of an old packing case as table. Flagon of beer between them.*)

BAILEY: Deal 'em.

(JEFF *lies down, paperback open, reading.* JACKO *shuffles pack, but he's still bothered about* JEFF. *He glares across at* JEFF. JEFF *sees him looking, shields his eyes from sun and gives* JACKO *a quizzical look, slowly gerns (pulls) a funny face.* JACKO *kicks some scuffling at him.*)

BAILEY: Hey! Less have the cards.

(JACKO *starts to deal cards, which happen to be the kind that have nude women, or partly clad women on the back in outrageously banal, provocative, or obscene poses. Of course the pack is much battered, and any picture would need to be stared at to make out what was on the back. But* BAILEY *stares holding one of the cards myopically up close.*)

ACT ONE 19

BAILEY: Christ!

JACKO: What's up?

BAILEY: I wish I could get my missus to take her knickers off like that.

JACKO: Yeah? And why can't you?

BAILEY: She don't go in for it like that.

JACKO: No?

BAILEY: I could never get her to pose with an apple in her ... like that one ... Not my Sheila ... Anyway, these days it's a matter of in, out, thanks a lot ...

JACKO: (*Grinning*) Bam Bam thank you, Mam.

BAILEY: Somepn of the sort.

JACKO: (*Still grinning*) That surprises me, Bailey. Man like you.

BAILEY: No. See. The trouble is. The trouble. Me. I'm too much for her. I'm over length (JACKO *snickers*). No. No codding. She went to see the quack, it seems. He told her. She's raw inside. Told me I gotta lay off, he says.

(BAILEY, *showing a surprising vulnerability and naivety in talking so openly, seems torn between being proud of being able to bring this about and genuine worry for his missus. He wishes he'd said nothing. He lays down card. Sort of disowning it.*)

BAILEY: Let's play cards.

JACKO: Don't you have a dabble?

BAILEY: (*Tetchy*) Ye'. Ye'. Course I do. Whatdya think? S'alright. I take it gently. Don't go at it like a beast. She gotta get somethin' out of it too. I know how to treat a woman. It's okay. (*Then, needing to boast to re-establish himself*). That's why she turns a blind eye when I spends a bit of time with this red-haired party up street. A man's got to have his full quota.

JACKO: Yep. True. Very true.

(JACKO *is about to add something to this when he hears* JEFF *chuckle. Both—*BAILEY *looking for a distraction—turn to look at him.*)

BAILEY: What's up with Punkie over there? What's he tittering about?

JACKO: He's just grown Big Ears. Tell Bailey what you're laughing at.

JEFF: Oh, it's a bit too facetious . . .

JACKO: Yeah? Well let's hear what you were being facetious all to yourself about.

BAILEY: Ye'. Out with it!

JEFF: (*Kidding gently. Thinking he's in with* BAILEY *and may be allowed.*) I was just wondering. Just passed through my mind. How this redhead up the street takes 'em off.

BAILEY: (*Mock hard. Not too seriously*) It's none of your business. But she takes 'em off sharp an' willingly, I tell you that.

JACKO: Ah, take no notice of him. He knows nothing yet.

BAILEY: No. He don't. Maybe we shoulda thrown him in the river after all.

JACKO: (*To* BAILEY, *after glaring round at* JEFF.) Your deal.

(BAILEY *deals.* JACKO, *the hard man, takes stump of cigarette from band of his trilby and lights up. He laughs.* BAILEY, *paranoid, suspecting a joke he's missed against himself, glares at* JACKO, *then at* JEFF *and back again.*)

BAILEY: Yes? Whatsamatter now?

JACKO: Reminds me of this joke. This fella, something like our Jeffrey here. In fact, now I come to think of it, it might have been our Jeffrey here. Yes, I was told, it was Jeffrey. Anyway, he takes his bird to the pictures, you know. He tried to get her home alone with the video when his ma was out, but she wouldn't wear it. So he takes her to the bug house. And the pictures one of these, you know . . . (*Makes a fist*) all in a shower,

ACT ONE

half a dozen of 'em all soapin' each other an' all that. Anyway, halfway through this really dirty bit where this bird's about to. . . .

JEFF: It's always halfway through, in these tales. Have you noticed?

JACKO: Shurrup.

JEFF: Why don't you learn a different story-telling technique?

JACKO: Shurrup! Right. Just shurrup! Halfway through where this bird's down on this other bird, Jeffie starts getting a bit over excited, he can't hold back, so he whips out his old man and he slips it in his bird's hand. "Oh, thanks very much," she says, "I'll put it behind me ear and smoke it later."

(JACKO *laughs much more than the joke merits. Turns to look at* JEFF. JEFF *smiles sweetly but tightly.*)

JACKO: Is that right, Jeff?

BAILEY: Well, I never, s'that right, Jeff?

JEFF: Anything Jacko says.

(JACKO, *kicking more scuffling at* JEFF. BAILEY, *turning over his cards, discards one, buys another from the pile.*)

BAILEY: Shit! Will you look at this one here. She got one like a horse collar.

JACKO: Reminds me o' the one I had up in town. Christ, man, a weekend with her an' I was seein' double . . .

BAILEY: Redhead, eh?

JACKO: Yeah, that's the sort to have—biting and scratching. This weekend I'm telling you about . . . she . . .

BAILEY: This party up the street. Did I tell you she's a redhead?

JACKO: Yeah, yeah, I think you said, but this bird of mine she . . .

BAILEY: Look at this.

(BAILEY *pulls down collar of his shirt, reveals supposedly woman-made scratches.* JACKO *whistles in feigned admiration so that* BAILEY *may be more ready to listen to his tale.*)

JACKO: Married is she?

BAILEY: He don' mind.

BAILEY: (*Disbelieving, but pretending to admire.*) Oh, ye' well . . . (*He whistles, what a great guy* BAILEY *is.*)

BAILEY: Knows him well. Drinks with him.

JACKO: Ye'?

BAILEY: Ye'.

JACKO: This bird I had in town was divorced. She . . .

BAILEY: He's a old guy, see. Nice chap. Nice chap.

JACKO: Ye! Well this bird's husband had been no good to her. She'd do anythin' for me. But I loved her and left her.

BAILEY: He's a damn good skin. But no good over the distance. Flags on the last furlong.

JACKO: No good up the back straight.

BAILEY: No good up the back straight. I do the guy a favor.

(JACKO *nods, understanding.*)

BAILEY: No good letting a good woman like he got go sour and stale. He appreciates it. An' she hangs on to me for grim death.

JACKO: Yeah, that's the type to have.

(BAILEY *takes a long sup of beer.*)

JACKO: I had a similar arrangement when I worked in this hotel on the coast, last summer.

BAILEY: (*Not interested*) Yeah, yeah.

JACKO: Yeah.

(JEFF, *fed up beyond amusement at listening to these two sexual boastings, gives a long, very audible yawn, stands up, walks to*

ACT ONE   23

edge of stage whistling extremely loudly and tunelessly. He then crouches on one knee, as if trying to attract attention of passing water fowl.)

BAILEY: What's the matter with young Jeff, again?

JACKO: Listening to the men talk is getting her frustrated.

BAILEY: You'll have your turn, Jeff.

JACKO: You think he's up to it?

BAILEY: We'll have to fix him up and find out.

JACKO: We'll get you a piece of togy soon, don't fret.

BAILEY: Then you can join in our twat jangling.

JACKO: Yeah, in the meantime you'll have to make do with the five-fingered widow. See, he was just about to slope off over there to visit it.

JEFF: Jacko, you are disgusting . . .

JACKO: And leave them ducks alone too . . .

JEFF: This one's got grease all over its feathers.

JACKO: Will have if it's left to you. See what he's up to, Bailey?

JEFF: This river really is a disgrace.

BAILEY: Caught my lad at home at it yesterday. Had all these porno books spread around his bed, away he was going like the clappers.

JACKO: What did you do?

BAILEY: Belted his earhole for him.

JACKO: It's the only way to learn 'em. You hear this, old fuck-a-duck?

JEFF: Give it a rest, Jacko.

(JACKO, *laughing—big man.* JEFF *is forced to laugh, too, at his inanities.*)

JACKO: (*Looking at his cards.*) Okay, I'll see you?

BAILEY: Sure?

JACKO: Come on. Lay 'em down.

BAILEY: Right, you asked for it.

(*They lay down cards.*)

JACKO: Shit! You jammy bugger.

(BAILEY, *laughing deeply, dirty, real heap-big man, pulls across cards and coins.*)

BAILEY: Double or quits.

JACKO: Okay.

BAILEY: I'll let you shuffle and deal.

(JACKO, *not looking happy. He hates losing, shuffles.* JEFF, *after watching the other two for a moment, looks as if he's going to move away, but fears comments if he does. Also, if he's honest he knows he's held by these two. Sort of fascinated, he sits down and opens up book again.*)

BAILEY: Where you got to in that book, boy?

JEFF: About halfway.

BAILEY: Has he had her yet?

JEFF: Several times. But that isn't what it's about.

JACKO: Yeah, what is it about?

JEFF: A young bloke fighting against the domination of his mother, but knowing he'll never really win, some mother or other will always have him . . .

JACKO: Tch! Incest!

BAILEY: S'all right. You gotta start somewhere. You begin at home and work out . . . I read a book by that feller you're reading there. Show us the cover? Yeah, that's him. All have the same cover. 'Tis a bird, in it?

JEFF: Phoenix.

BAILEY: Yeah, I see it now. Yeah, same bloke.

JEFF: You read D.H. Lawrence?

JACKO: You ain't the only one to read you know, smart arse.

JEFF: Yes, what have you read, Jacko?

JACKO: Me? All sorts.

JEFF: Like what?

JACKO: Christ, I told you. All sorts. Poetry . . .

JEFF: You?

JACKO: Yes, I read poetry. Had this bird who was keen on it. Always reading it she was. And there was this one good poet she always read.

JEFF: Who?

JACKO: Name me a poet?

JEFF: Lawrence.

JACKO: Na.

JEFF: Hardy, T.S. Eliot, Shakespeare, e.e. cummings, Ginsberg, Snyder, Chaucer, Dryden, Milton, Dylan Thomas, Sylvia Plath, Ted Hughes, Stevie Smith, John Donne, Andrew Marvell . . .

JACKO: Na, none o' that crap. Name me a real poet.

JEFF: Er . . . well . . .

JACKO: Come on smart arse, supposed to be so smart? Begins with K.

JEFF: Keats.

JACKO: That's him. Keats. He's great. "I wandered lonely as a cloud . . . ."

JEFF: That isn't . . . Well, . . . (*He decides not to correct Jacko.*)

JACKO: "A thing of beauty is a joy for ever."

JEFF: Yes.

JACKO: "I met a lady in the fucking meads . . ." That's Keats. That's great, you think, I know nothing.

JEFF: I never said that. I think, to be honest, you do yourself an injustice . . .

JACKO: I even write poetry . . . Wanna hear some . . . There was a young bugger called Jeff/Who when it came to sex was quite neff. . . .

BAILEY: This book I read by that guy there . . . He had this part where this lady of the manor puts a daisy chain around this bloke's cock.

JACKO: Gerraway.

BAILEY: Yes, I remember. Read it back years ago when I was in the army . . .

JACKO: Jeeze, I'd like to meet a lady o' the manor like that. She wouldn't get chance to do no daisy chaining. . . .

BAILEY: Then there was this other book. About this ass. Used put him on show with a woman . . .

JEFF: The Golden Ass . . . Apuleius.

BAILEY: Yes, I seen that for real. Out in the Middle East. They has this donkey up on this cradle and they has this woman laid out and they lowers the donkey down . . .

JACKO: Christ she must have some delve to take a . . .

BAILEY: He can only go so far. They has this brass ring round it, so he can't go too far . . .

JACKO: Maybe that's what you need, Bailey . . .

BAILEY: Yes, I read all sorts in my time. Not all of it sex. I read some good books too. But I don't read much now. I mean you can't take any notice what these writers tell you, most of 'em are a lot of lazy faggots. Poofters who don't wanna work. They haven't done what they write about most of 'em . . .

JEFF: The best ones have. Hemingway, he did. *A Farewell to Arms. The Sun Also Rises.* Great stuff. He lived all that. Lawrence, he lived it. It's all in *Mr. Noon*, and this book here . . .

BAILEY: I did some gardening for a writer once. Miserable, phony bleeder he was. Always pissed. Always posing. Mean. Tight as a frog's arse.

JEFF: Couldn't have been any good.

BAILEY: Worked at the University. Touched up his students on the side.

JEFF: No artist worth his salt can be mean, or lack humanity. If he does he isn't worth bothering with . . .

JACKO: Trouble with you, Jeff, you're green. You think everybody should think like you . . .

BAILEY: But I don't read much now . . .

JEFF: It's the thing that's kept me sane. . . .

BAILEY: Hurts my eyes. The print. So small nowadays.

JACKO: Whyn't you get glasses?

BAILEY: Me? In glasses? I look like Dagwood Bumstead.

JACKO: (*To* JEFF) An' all this stuff about ladies of the manor goin' around putting daisy chains on blokes' knollucks is in this book you're reading now?

JEFF: Not specifically, but . . .

JACKO: What does your ma say about you bringin' books like that in the house?

JEFF: What can she say?

BAILEY: Couldn't have books like that in our house. My missus'd kick yer arse for you.

JACKO: Deserve it, too. Dirty gett, Jeff, with books like that. Your lay, Bailey.

BAILEY: (*Starting at back of card.*) Ye', I'm just thinking about it.

JACKO: (*To* JEFF) Lend it to me when you've finished with it.

BAILEY: I'll buy that card.

JACKO: Okay, there you go. Got you this time, I'm thinkin'.

BAILEY: Will you look at her, Jesus.

JACKO: Tasty. Definitely tasty.

(JEFF *gives up trying to read. Stares into river.*)

BAILEY: Whatsa matter, kid. You look really chocka.

JEFF: I am. Yes.

JACKO: Yeah, he's chocka. Look at him. Poor little sod, he's really beat.

(*Silence as card players carry on with their game.* JEFF *stands, goes to edge of river bank. He hopes the others do not make any more ribald comments.* BAILEY *looks over at him. He becomes a little more mellow, a little more kind. Nods to* JACKO *that he, too, should take it easy.*)

BAILEY: What's getting you down, son? You don't want to take too much notice of us, you know. Don't take what we say too seriously. That's what's wrong with you, you try to take us too seriously. We just gas the way we do to pass the time over. We get our time over that's all. An' after a mornin' in that hell-hole back there, we have to sound off to make ourselves feel a bit more human. We're both a couple of piss and wind merchants, if we're honest. So don't take us so seriously. Especially this fella here. He talks a load of rubbish . . .

JACKO: (*Easier, friendly*) Wass mean? Course he has to take notice of me. Where would he be without me? I'm his big cocker daddy? Here, Kiddo, have a sip o' your daddy's beer.

JEFF: No. It's okay. But thanks.

BAILEY: Go on, kid. Jungle juice that. Do you good.

JEFF: No. Thanks. I'd be asleep all afternoon over my machine.

JACKO: (*Still matey*) Yeah, you were bad enough this mornin' when you came in, weren't you? I looked at you. Didn't you see him, Bailey. His eyes were down here on his cheek bones. I looked at you, Jeff, an' thought, this fella's not going to have the strength to switch his machine on this mornin' never mind do any more work. Jesus, I thought, I'm going to be carrying him again. I've carried him for the last week.

JEFF: I was reading til late.

JACKO: Yeah, we know. You wanna go to bed with boxing gloves on, sort o' books you read . . .

(JACKO *laughs, but a bit more gently as* BAILEY *signals that perhaps they should take it easy with* JEFF. *He can't take it.*)

JACKO: Easy, Jeff.

(JEFF *stands with hands tucked in his belt and trousers top, staring down into water.*)

BAILEY: Don't be too chocka, boy. Not that bad. What's up?

JACKO: You got us. We're your mates. Wass up wi' yer?

JEFF: Ah.

JACKO: Really chocka then, Jeff, are you? Come on, tell your Daddy Jacko all about it.

BAILEY: Ye', come on, kid.

(*Silence. Then an outburst from* JEFF.)

JEFF: Ah, I get bloody sick of it here.

JACKO: Bloody frustrated is all you are

BAILEY: (*To* JACKO) Easy.

JEFF: (*Angry*) I'm full up to here. Sick. Day like this and having to go back into that works. This isn't life. There's got to be better than this. All that stink. Noise. Dirt in there. Like you said. We aren't human. No wonder you have to talk so . . . I'd like to get in my old jalopy and drive off into the hills this afternoon. Over through the woods. Call in home first for the dog. She's lovely. I love just to watch her run through the woods, sniffing in amongst all the undergrowth. She's fully alive when she's out. I know this pond up in the hills. The other side of the woods. Nobody goes there.

Crystal clear. Fish in it. Carp. And you can swim in it. I have swum in it. In bare pelt. Lie out on the rocks. Peaceful. When you whistle or sing out, it echoes. That's where I'd be this afternoon. Not back in there. I could love my life if I had the chance. Wouldn't waste it. And the fella who owns the place, where's he today? Three-hour lunch. Getting pissed up at the country club. Comes back drunk as a skunk. Sees nothing of what's around him.

BAILEY: You know, a fella who reads like you, and all that. Good school you went to . . .

JEFF: Only went to grammar school.

JACKO: (*Tetchy*) Way you go on, you make it sound you went to Oxford . . .

BAILEY: Better school than the one I went to anyway. You ought to get a good job . . .

JEFF: Grammar school isn't anything. You soon learn that . . .

JACKO: Reads the wrong sort of books, anyroad.

BAILEY: It's what you make of yourself . . .

JEFF: I did have a good job once. Great. My first job. Worked with this old guy. We used to go around renovating churches. Patching up and refashioning statuary, things like that. There used to be some beautiful old churches round here. Full of beautiful carvings. Stone work . . .

BAILEY: You can't beat those old craftsmen. We've got nothing like them now . . .

JEFF: This old guy I worked with was good. He knew every trick there was. He could render a piece of stone and make it just look like the way it was in the Middle Ages. It used to be so peaceful working in the churches, sun shining in through the stained glass, it was like being in a different century . . .

JACKO: Churches give me the creeps sometimes.

ACT ONE

JEFF: Sometimes a church would be being closed down, so we used to take things to be preserved in the church museum. I sometimes go and look at them now . . .

JACKO: But I worked as a grave digger once, and it was surprising what we found in them graves . . .

BAILEY: Why d'you pack the job in if you liked it so much?

JEFF: The old guy died. The job finished. Nobody else took it on. They let the old churches fall down, or they turn 'em into fitness centers, or people with money buy them and do 'em out to live in. They become video centers, or they become warehouses, or something. Nobody cares now. That's why everything is such shit. (*He stops, surprised at himself for saying so much, becoming so emotional. He concludes.*) Think, I might get myself a job on a farm.

BAILEY: No bloody money in that . . .

JACKO: No money in any of that.

JEFF: I don't give a damn for money.

BAILEY: Hey, don't say that. You gotta cross yourself when you say that. Money's sacred now.

JEFF: Not to me.

JACKO: This is the only place where there's any money round here. I've worked all over the place in these parts. Useless. This is the only place for money. In fact. It's the only place you can get a job at all.

BAILEY: True. He's right. Got to thank Christ you even got a job.

JACKO: Right.

JEFF: Well, I don't thank anybody for me having to give up the only life I'll ever know—because don't get me wrong, I'm not going religious on you. I can't believe in God or life after death or any of that malarky, I just liked the church buildings . . .

BAILEY: (*Showing crucifix*) Should be ashamed of yourself. I believe in God.

JACKO: Ye', so do I.

JEFF: Well, I believe we've only got one life and it's tragic we have to spend it on this garbage. Putting up with the shit we have to put up with fills me with pain. I'm gonna split altogether soon. Get a Land Rover. Clear off.

(*Silence*)

JACKO: Yeah, I'm thinking of pissing off back to town. More life there.

BAILEY: (*Suddenly angry*) Look, are we playing cards or aren't we?

JACKO: (*Also angry*) It's this fella's fault. Whingeing away there nuff to give yer the shits. (*To* JEFF) Look, if it's as bad as that, get yourself off behind those bushes and get rid of it . . .

JEFF: (*Depressed again*) Bloody useless trying to talk to you, Jacko. Might have known . . .

BAILEY: (*Slams down cards.*) Got you again.

JACKO: (*Tetchier than ever*) Sodding jammy bugger again.

(BAILEY *laughs his deep laugh, pulls the coins in, big man, as in the westerns.*)

BAILEY: Another round?

JACKO: (*Hunching forward*) No. Fuck it.

(JACKO *sits sourly staring at the ground. He looks at* JEFF, *angry with him for raising a few questions. He draws a pattern in the dust with a stick. A quick caricature of* JEFF. *Lewd maybe, but very good.* BAILEY *looks over and laughs.* JACKO *rubs out drawing with his foot. All lapse into boredom.* JEFF *sits silently.*)

JACKO: (*Starting to sing*) Jeffrey is a lazy coon.
He don't wanna work in the afternoon.
Off to the woods I seed him go.
Wagglin' his fagin to and fro . . .
Along comes a bee . . . Buzz Buzz Bee . . .

ACT ONE

JEFF: Shut up, Jacko. Shut up.

BAILEY: Yes!

(JACKO *ignores them both and continues singing as he reaches over and takes a mouth organ from the pocket of his slung-down denim jacket.*)

JACKO: Get away from me you bumble bee
I ain't no rose,
I ain't no pretty little flower,
Get off my fucking nose . . .

BAILEY: I told you lay off or I'll . . .

(JACKO, *about to put mouth organ to his lips, stops and looks across river.*)

(*A spotlight has been coming up on the edge of Stage One. Into the spotlight comes* ANGELA. *She holds invoice in hand. She affects to be just looking through window, taking a breather, seems only interested in the scenery and is oblivious of the men below.* JEFF *sees where* JACKO *is looking. Both keep their attention on the house across the river,* JACKO's *jaw has dropped open. He tilts back his trilby to have a proper look.* BAILEY, *who has been about to grab* JACKO *to warn him to do as he tells him, stops and glares at* JACKO.)

JACKO: Bird.

BAILEY: Prick.

JACKO: No. Honest. In that house over the water. Like he said. I've been keeping my eye out for them and there they are.

BAILEY: Don't you start.

JACKO: Straight up. Look yourself.

BAILEY: Bollocks.

JACKO: Turn round and see. (*Calling to* ANGELA.) Hello, darlin'.

BAILEY: You havin' me on. . . ? (*He begins to turn.*) If you've havin' me on . . . (*And by the time he's turned around* ANGELA *has withdrawn; the light has gone out.*)

JACKO: (*To* JEFF) Thought you was kidding us before.

JEFF: Told you.

BAILEY: (*Having missed* ANGELA, *is turning on* JACKO.) Jacko, you arsehole.

JACKO: There is a bird over there. (*To* JEFF) Tell him.

BAILEY: Jeff?

JEFF: Yes, it's right.

BAILEY: You'll both go in the river in a minute if you piss up my back . . .

JACKO: Telling you . . . (*He's about to put mouth organ to his lips.* BAILEY *knocks it from his hand into the dust.*). He . . . ey, what you do that for . . . ? You ruined it . . . Get dust in it . . .

BAILEY: Take the piss out of me you'll get dust up where the sun don't shine . . .

JACKO: (*Retrieving his mouth organ.*) This bird at the window over there. Big Bubs on her.

BAILEY: Crumpet on the brain you have, Jacko. Problie a mirage you saw.

(JACKO *shrugs, pulls down brim of his trilby, holds mouth organ in his hand.* JEFF *has stood up and is at the edge of river bank.*)

(JACKO *pokes mouth organ with stick, bangs it to get dust out of it.* BAILEY, *even more frustrated and bored, sups beer and looks at backs of playing cards, the study of which does him no good at all.*)

BAILEY: (*After a groan of anguish.*) Holy Mother, I'm gonna start going home for me dinner again.

(JACKO *gives a sudden burst of laughter.* BAILEY *glares savagely at* JACKO. *Then, with a slow owning-up smile, passes across playing cards to* JACKO.)

JACKO: You coulda borried me bike if it hadn't been in dock.

(BAILEY *grins, shrugs. It was just a thought.* BAILEY *takes cigarettes from shirt pocket, selects one, puts it between his lips, tosses packet across to* JACKO, *who takes one, puts it between his lips, and tosses packet back.* BAILEY, *about to put packet away, thinks again, offers a cigarette to* JEFF, *who shakes his head.* BAILEY *puts packet in pocket.* JACKO *lights match on seat of his trousers.* BAILEY *nonchalantly flicks his alight with his finger nail. They smoke their cigarettes,* BAILEY *sleepily.* JACKO *has one last look at the cards, kisses the top one lewdly, tongues it.* BAILEY *watches him.*)

BAILEY: That'll be the day.

JACKO: I done worse than that, with better than this.

BAILEY: In your dreams.

JACKO: To join the Chapter I had to do more than that in front of Witnesses.

BAILEY: (*Aimlessly*) Tch! Witnesses! I'd a gone through all the Witnesses an' all. 'Spect theyda had to make me high priest or somepn. (*He laughs quickly.*) Eh, Jeff? (*When* JEFF *doesn't reply he glares around.*) I said . . .

(*He stops on seeing where* JEFF *is looking.* JACKO *also looks up.*)

(*Spotlight has come on again on the edge of Stage One. Into spotlight this time comes* JUDITH. *She does not look out. She has only come over to window to pick up a fresh batch of invoices.*)

JACKO: Look.

BAILEY: That her?

JACKO: See!

BAILEY: Jeeze.

JACKO: That's a different one. There must be two of them.

BAILEY: She's all right.

JEFF: (*Despite himself*) Yes, she's nice.

JACKO: Na, not as good as the other one. She's a cracker the other one. See, there she is. Look. Look. Looka dat! Woooowooo.

(*Now* ANGELA *has come into spotlight on Stage One, a checklist in hand as if in conference with* JUDITH. *The two stand still a moment. Then* JUDITH *turns away out of spot light to go further back into office, out of view.* ANGELA *remains at window, seeming to be very casual.*)

JACKO: WoooooWooooow.

BAILEY: Yarbooool Yay Yay.... (*Stomps his feet.*)

JACKO: Jesus! If I could get to that one. If I had me bike I'd get to that one. Over the bridge, brrrm brrrm.

BAILEY: Yeah, yeah, yeah.

(BAILEY *goes to edge of stage, begins stripping off his shirt, flexing his muscles, generally stomping.* JACKO *strips off his t-shirt.*)

(JEFF *shakes his head, half grins, 'Here they go again,' but he licks his lips, doesn't quite know what to do. He wishes he wasn't with* BAILEY *and* JACKO, *but he can't leave.*)

(BAILEY *and* JACKO *start whistling and shouting—"Here yar darlin'! Over here!"—and the like.*)

(ANGELA *remains in spotlight, but still doesn't look across the river.*)

(*Start to fade down lights on Stage Two, retain spotlight on Stage One.*)

(*Blackout Stage Two completely, leaving only sounds and shouts of* BAILEY *and* JACKO (*on tape*).)

Scene Three

(*Lights up fully on Stage One.*)

(JUDITH *is at desk.* ANGELA, *laughing, is walking toward desk, enjoying the impression she's made on the men below.*)

(*The shouts and whistles of* BAILEY *and* JACKO *are just faintly audible from across the river. They fade out completely so as not to be intrusive during the next scene.*)

Act One

ANGELA: Listen to that lot.

JUDITH: Yes.

ANGELA: Terrible, aren't they?

JUDITH: Yes.

ANGELA: I'm not codding you, you only have to show yourself at the window and they go crackers.

JUDITH: Yes, you do.

ANGELA: Terrible lot.

JUDITH: Yes. Here, I've got all this bumph into company and date order. I'll call them out again. We'll do each company in turn (ANGELA *is sidling over to window again whilst* JUDITH *is talking.*) and then we'll make a grand total of all we've done so far. (*She stops talking when she sees that* ANGELA *is on tiptoe, peeping out of window.*) Do you agree?

ANGELA: Uh?

JUDITH: We'll try for a grand total.

ANGELA: Oh. Oh. Yes.

JUDITH: Then that's what we'll do shall we?

ANGELA: Oh, oh, yes.

JUDITH: Kippers this year are in short supply

ANGELA: Oh. Yes.

JUDITH: But tomatoes are coming down in price.

ANGELA: All right.

JUDITH: But the sun shines bright just the same.

ANGELA: Yes.

JUDITH: Listen, do you want to get finished up here and get home or not?

ANGELA: Wha'?

JUDITH: I thought we agreed to work through lunch and finish up today. . . . (*She shrugs. Obviously she's going to have to wait until* ANGELA *is ready.*) Oh, well . . . Never mind . . . There are obviously more important things to consider. . . .

ANGELA: (*As if watching the antics of monkeys at the zoo.*) Awwwww look at 'em, look. They're showing off. Bless 'em. Loook at 'em.

JUDITH: (*Standing to look over at window.*) I can imagine.

ANGELA: No. Come and see. It's a treat.

(JUDITH *goes over to window, arms folded, looks down.*)

ANGELA: What a lot.

JUDITH: That's what they're doing, all right. Showing off.

ANGELA: And they know we're watching them.

JUDITH: The know *you* are watching them.

ANGELA: (*A wry dig*) Oh, ah, an' what are you doing?

JUDITH: Uh! (*She turns away quickly, holds herself more tightly, then stops.*)

ANGELA: (*Smiling*) Ah, bless 'em.

(*She remains at window, smiling.* JUDITH *moves back into office and then goes back to window.*)

ANGELA: Look. They're doing handstands.

JUDITH: (*Lips tense*) Mmmm.

ANGELA: All that flesh. Not bad though, is it?

JUDITH: Mmmmmm.

ANGELA: (*Quietly*) Be honest now, admit it.

JUDITH: Mmmm. I've seen worse.

ANGELA: That older bloke, he's got quite a good body, on him, an 'e? All that hairy chest and that. He's the one who's got the er . . . You know he's . . .

JUDITH: Quite well favored.

ANGELA: Quite well favored! Like a bleedn tent pole. He could do you an injury.

Act One

JUDITH: (*Drily*) You wouldn't need a scrape . . .

ANGELA: (*Laughing loudly at* JUDITH's *unexpectedly waggish—for her—comment.*) No, you bleddy wouldn't. How they get 'em that long . . .

JUDITH: I believe they hang weights on them.

ANGELA: Na, go'way. That true.

JUDITH: Or pack them with a Growmore poultice.

ANGELA: Na? Ah, you're sending me up.

JUDITH: Shall we get on with some work?

ANGELA: Eh? Oh, ah. Hey, you got to admit. There's a couple o' good bods down there, hey? I mean it sends you a bit gooey, dun it? Hey, I mean it's got to be the same for you as it is for me and like it is for them. Or I mean is it just me who's got a bit too much of the randy in her?

JUDITH: It's a matter of type. If you like the type. I think we fall for types.

ANGELA: Well, I don't go a lot on the type on display down there, but they look all right. I mean that one there, that fella has the trilby, he looks all right, and he knows it, too . . .

JUDITH: So does the other one.

ANGELA: The older guy?

JUDITH: Yes. He's pretty vain.

ANGELA: They never grow out of it.

JUDITH: No.

ANGELA: That little one's nice.

JUDITH: Yes, I wonder if he's as bad as the rest.

ANGELA: Oh, see the old bloke, see the way he moves about. Look. Watch him now. He's walking across there, pretending he's looking for something. See the way he swaggers. Belly sucked in. Chest out. Arse stuck out too. Bleddy funny.

JUDITH: Yes... He reminds me of someone . . . I . . . er . . .

ANGELA: Look at the other one. See, he's holding his belly in too so he don't show his little beer pot, tho' to be fair he ain't got much of a pot . . . Ah, but look at this little one though. He wants to get into the act now. He's stripping down to his trunks, too . . . See him . . .

JUDITH: Yes, I do.

ANGELA: Hey, he ain't bad stripped. He's got a good leg on him, like a footballer. Nice tight little bum. See . . .

JUDITH: Yes.

ANGELA: That un there with the trilby. He keeps sort of getting at the little one. Grabbing at him. You know? Acting like a dog. You know? Yeah, he thinks he's it that one with the trilby. He had a motor bike. Bit of a Hells Angel. 'Sept he was usually on his own. A lone wolf. But he nearly killed hisself on this motor bike. He was in court a bit back. He looks all right, but he's a bit dodgy. Look at him now, showing off. Lifting that stone. They're all showing off. Ah, bless 'em. And it's all for us.

JUDITH: Yes.

ANGELA: In it funny tho'?

JUDITH: It's interesting.

ANGELA: Bleddy funny.

JUDITH: Quite an exhibition.

ANGELA: All for us.

JUDITH: Do you think we should applaud?

ANGELA: No, they might come round with the hat.

JUDITH: They might . . .

ANGELA: Let's just enjoy it. It's better than the telly, this.

ACT ONE 41

JUDITH: Yes, but we do have work to do. Let's get it done.

(*She moves back to desk.* ANGELA *doesn't move.*)

(*Spotlight comes on on edge of Stage Two.*)

(JACKO *and* BAILEY *are giving their strange stomping and muscle flexing routine. A kind of ritual game. Then* JEFF *joins in. His muscles, strangely enough, seem the better toned. They form a sort of tableau.*)

JUDITH: Angela.

(ANGELA *reluctantly leaves window and goes across to table.*)

(*The spotlight goes out over men on Stage Two.*)

(*The whistles and rooster calls of the men continue. Again, as before, these sounds subside as the scene between* ANGELA *and* JUDITH *continues. The women, both in their own way, seem a little more thoughtful, subdued at first.*)

JUDITH: Ready for me to begin calling the figures out?

ANGELA: (*Quietly*) Yes.

JUDITH: Okay, here we go . . .

ANGELA: Eyes down for a full house.

JUDITH: Forty-four pounds thirty-six . . .

ANGELA: Just a minid . . .

JUDITH: What?

ANGELA: Nose started running again.

(*She blows nose on Kleenex, slings soiled tissue toward basket.* JUDITH *sighs, gives her a look.*)

ANGELA: Thought it was clearing up.

JUDITH: Forty-four pounds thirty-six . . . Oh, wait a minute, these invoices have got out of order. Hang fire a sec.

ANGELA: Funny aren't they, blokes? Doesn't take much to set'em off. They only need to catch sight of someone and they're away. I sometimes try to get it out of my fiancé what he's like when I'm not around, when he's with his mates. He'll never say. He cracks on, butter wouldn't melt in his mouth.

JUDITH: Perhaps it wouldn't.

ANGELA: It better wouldn't. I mean if I catches him shouting and whistling after girls like them down there I'll have his Adam's apple for a bottle stopper. But the thing about him, though, is he's so jealous.

JUDITH: I don't know many who aren't.

ANGELA: What's sauce for the goose is sauce for the gander as far as I'm concerned . . .

JUDITH: (*With invoices in front of her.*) I think we're about ready again now . . .

ANGELA: Don't think I'm nosey . . .

JUDITH: What?

ANGELA: But I couldn't help noticing you're not wearing a ring or anything.

JUDITH: Not now. No.

ANGELA: You're not married?

JUDITH: Not now.

ANGELA: You were once? I mean, I'm not being nosey.

JUDITH: Yes. I was married once. Let's start again. Forty-four pounds thirty-six . . .

ANGELA: What happened.

JUDITH: I'm sorry?

ANGELA: What happened? When you were married?

JUDITH: Nothing happened.

ANGELA: For you not to be married . . .

JUDITH: Well, it did happen for a while, then it stopped. Which is why I'm no longer married.

ANGELA: I'm sorry.

JUDITH: No need for you to be sorry. Not exactly unique

these days, is it? (*She indicates she's ready to work. She doesn't really want to talk any more.*)

ANGELA: Do you miss it?

JUDITH: I er . . . beg your pardon?

ANGELA: Do you miss it?

JUDITH: What?

ANGELA: You know.

JUDITH: Not the faintest.

ANGELA: Being married.

JUDITH: Like a sore thumb.

ANGELA: Honest?

JUDITH: (*Pausing, after some thought.*) Well, yes, I suppose if I'm honest, I do miss it from time to time. I must admit, on a hot day and . . .

ANGELA: Ah, ah, I get you you're being a bit . . .

JUDITH: I'm sorry I didn't mean to be so crude . . .

ANGELA: Oh, don't mind me, I like a bit of a joke. I can't stand these people who have no sense of humor. I'm all for a laugh, aren't you?

JUDITH: Up to a point.

ANGELA: I don't mind a point now and then either . . .

JUDITH: When it's in our favor.

ANGELA: Hey, you're quite rum aren't you? I mean you're all right. I was a bit worried about you, you know you talk so posh and that and you have posh ways but I mean I bet you could be a laugh . . .

JUDITH: Yes.

ANGELA: Do you ever see him?

JUDITH: My ex-husband?

ANGELA: Do you see him sometimes?

JUDITH: He's already with someone else.

ANGELA: Oh.

JUDITH: Yes.

ANGELA: Did you used to fancy him a lot?

JUDITH: Yes. Quite a lot, I suppose . . . I . . .

ANGELA: And what do you feel like when you see him now?

JUDITH: I . . . I . . . don't really know . . . I . . . Shall we get on?

ANGELA: Only, I've often wondered what it must be like when you're used to being with someone, sleeping with them, getting used to what they do, then you split up. Do you still have the same feelings?

JUDITH: Sometimes. It comes and goes.

ANGELA: Do you think of him with someone else?

JUDITH: Not the one he's with, no.

ANGELA: Who is she?

JUDITH: She used to be one of his students.

ANGELA: Teacher? Your husband?

JUDITH: Lecturer.

ANGELA: Lecherer?

JUDITH: That too.

ANGELA: At the University?

JUDITH: We both were.

ANGELA: Why did you leave?

JUDITH: I thought it best at the time.

ANGELA: I wouldn't have.

JUDITH: I was disturbed. Confused. I just wanted to get out. It was embarrassing all round. Especially as he was head of his faculty. A fuss might have destroyed his career and we'd both worked so hard on his career . . .

ACT ONE

ANGELA: Bugger that.

JUDITH: I was being sarcastic.

ANGELA: Yes, but you still left. I wouldn't have. I'd have said, "Listen here, matey, it's you who's causing all the bother, so why should I suffer and give up my job. You piss off with your little whore, I'm staying."

JUDITH: We were all being so civilized.

ANGELA: Bugger that.

JUDITH: It was put to me, by several people, that he was a rising star in the educational firmament, it would be wrong of me and very mean spirited to shoot him down. It was up to me to show maturity. Everyone would applaud me for it . . .

ANGELA: An' he stays where he is an' you end up here slavin' yer paps off in this boring hole.

JUDITH: It got me out of a jam. It's given me time to think.

ANGELA: But why did you stand for it? I wouldn't have stood for it.

JUDITH: I felt guilty, I suppose.

ANGELA: Arseholes.

JUDITH: Quite.

ANGELA: Stuff feeling guilty . . .

JUDITH: You don't understand.

ANGELA: He was in the wrong, you feel guilty?

JUDITH: I spoiled his plans.

ANGELA: What plans?

JUDITH: We had it all mapped out. We would have no children for a while. I would do all I could to help him up the ladder. Our joint salary would help build our home. My salary would also allow us to do the required amount of entertaining to help his rise . . .

ANGELA: Sucking round his bosses.

JUDITH: Polite politics . . .

ANGELA: Same thing . . .

JUDITH: Then when he'd achieved a suitable grade and had published his first book, I was to step down and have children. That was the plan, and I spoiled it.

ANGELA: Why? How?

JUDITH: I found I couldn't have children.

ANGELA: Might have been his fault.

JUDITH: I kept having miscarriages. It seemed pretty certain it was me.

ANGELA: You don't know. Try again with someone else.

JUDITH: It got a bit dangerous. We had a family discussion, a mature consultation . . .

ANGELA: Then he ditched you?

JUDITH: I was allowed to leave the marital home.

ANGELA: Because you couldn't have children?

JUDITH: It would be a shame if his genes and his brains were not passed on.

ANGELA: What about yours?

JUDITH: It doesn't matter . . .

ANGELA: Bloody monster. And he's supposed to educate people?

JUDITH: It's pretty average behavior these days . . .

ANGELA: And he's with this other girl now?

JUDITH: It hasn't stopped him wanting to come round to see me on the quiet, as he's so often lonely . . .

ANGELA: Lonely? How come he's lonely? I thought . . .

JUDITH: Well recently his student wife had her dissertation to complete. She demanded total silence. Right after that she started her first novel. I believe, too, that she's been commissioned by a friend of hers at the studios for her first telly play. So what with her committee work they don't get an awful lot of time together. And he doesn't get the attention he craves . . .

ANGELA: Serves him right . . . What's she write about anyroad?

JUDITH: Sisterhood?

ANGELA: I wouldn't like a sister like her . . .

JUDITH: Sisterhood, sharing and being honest. She's quite an expert. Everywhere you go these days you have her opinions foisted on you.

ANGELA: What the hell does she know?

JUDITH: Nothing. But it's funny how good and true causes always attract people who haven't a clue to pontificate on its behalf. Other people listen because it suits their purpose. No one ever seems to consider the damage they do to the causes they're supposed to be supporting . . .

ANGELA: Doesn't it make you sick?

JUDITH: Life's full of these little ironies.

ANGELA: You're too easy on her. I'd break her neck . . . But, how do you treat *him* when he comes round?

JUDITH: Like a sister.

ANGELA: Does he try it on? You know?

JUDITH: I do know.

ANGELA: Does he?

JUDITH: More than try.

ANGELA: What he . . .?

JUDITH: Came round one night plastered out of his mind.

ANGELA: And he . . . you mean . . . Christ! I wouldn't have any bloke doing that to me. Not less I wanted it . . .

JUDITH: He was very apologetic afterwards. Said he knew I'd understand. He was desperate, you see...

ANGELA: What a rotten bastard. Christ! It makes you...

JUDITH: (*Realizing she's said too much.*) Let's leave it now, eh?

ANGELA: When he calmed down after it, I mean, did you, er...

JUDITH: Angela, I've gone as far as I wish on the subject. Let's get this work done, shall we?

ANGELA: I mean...

JUDITH: If you don't mind.

ANGELA: Look, I'm not being nosey.

JUDITH: Then let's leave it alone, shall we? I've said as much as I want...

ANGELA: Okay, be like that...

JUDITH: Please try to understand... I... it's still... very... Oh, let's get on with some work . . . please...

ANGELA: No need to get edgy...

JUDITH: I just feel...

ANGELA: If you didn't want to talk about it you should have said.

JUDITH: Please.

ANGELA: I didn't mean to pry...

JUDITH: Very well then, let's...

ANGELA: Just a minid... (*She blows her nose in tissue, tosses it carelessly to basket.*)

JUDITH: (*Already raw, angered*) Look, why don't you think to put those handkerchiefs in a plastic bag.

ANGELA: (*Stung. Surprised.*) Wha'?

JUDITH: What? You heard what I said. I don't want to catch your germs...

ACT ONE

ANGELA: Very fussy aren't you?

JUDITH: If you blow your nose you bring out germs. If you just throw them willy nilly around the office as you have for the past couple of days you spread germs.

ANGELA: Gotta blow me nose an' I?

JUDITH: Granted, but put them in a plastic bag . . .

ANGELA: No need to . . . be so . . .

JUDITH: Didn't your mother ever teach you anything?

ANGELA: Listen here, I don't have to take that from you.

JUDITH: I don't want to catch your cold.

ANGELA: You're not my mother.

JUDITH: I'm damn thankful I'm not.

ANGELA: Who do you think you are?

JUDITH: Look . . . I'm sorry, but . . .

ANGELA: No bloody wonder your old man threw you . . .

JUDITH: Just be careful what you are saying . . .

ANGELA: Well . . .

JUDITH: Just don't say another word . . .

ANGELA: I . . .

JUDITH: I've warned you.

ANGELA: You're sorry you told me what you did now, aren't you?

JUDITH: You caught me on a bad day.

ANGELA: You shouldn't have told me if you . . .

JUDITH: I don't get much chance to talk to anyone these days.

ANGELA: That's not my fault.

JUDITH: I didn't say it was.

ANGELA: Don't blame me.

JUDITH: I'm not blaming you.

ANGELA: No need to take it out on me.

JUDITH: I'm not taking it out on you.

ANGELA: An' I can't help having a cold.

JUDITH: Just put your soiled tissues in a plastic bag and I'll be happy.

ANGELA: There isn't one.

JUDITH: Here, around the invoices . . .

ANGELA: Ta . . .

JUDITH: It's just that I can't afford to lose time from work with a cold as we don't get paid for time off. I've got rent to pay and . . .

ANGELA: Cold's nearly over now, anyway.

JUDITH: Well, all right, then . . .

(*Pause. Both sit silently. Not speaking for a moment.*)

(ANGELA *goes over to window. From a bag she takes out a flask, pours coffee into a cup.*)

(JUDITH *takes over adding machine and works on her own.*)

(*Full lights on Stage One change.* ANGELA *and* JUDITH *remain in individual spotlights.*)

(*Light comes up slowly on Stage Two: The River Bank.*)

(BAILEY *and* JEFF *sunbathe, lying flat.* JACKO *is sitting on his own on a log at the water's edge. He is very still. All the banter is over with for the moment. All the top show has gone, and what is underneath is quiet and melancholy.*)

(*Slowly, and without appearing conscious of what he is doing,* JACKO *puts the mouth organ to his lips. He plays a series of long, slow notes. They are so melancholy and blue and contain so much feeling that* JEFF *turns his head, shielding his eyes from the sun to stare over at* JACKO. *He looks over at* BAILEY, *who nods as if to say, 'Yes, I know.' But* JACKO, *oblivious to* JEFF, *continues to play.*)

(ANGELA, *at window of office, stops pouring coffee to listen.*
JUDITH *pauses a moment and listens.*)

(*These few notes on* JACKO's *mouth organ seem to encapsulate the feelings of all and the mood of this particular summer's day. Lights go out completely on Stage One.*)

(JACKO *becoming aware that* JEFF *is looking at him and listening to his playing, is embarrassed at the amount of genuine emotion he believes he has betrayed unawares. He stops playing.*)

JACKO: What are you looking at, Bugger Lugs?

JEFF: Hey, that's great, Jacko.

BAILEY: (*Lazily*) Ye', you're another one who's wasting his time hanging around here . . .

JACKO: Booooolll . . . Sheeet.

JEFF: No, that was good. Don't pull it down. That was really . . . Where d'you learn to play like that?

JACKO: (*Blowing spittle from mouth organ, putting it back in pocket of denim jacket.*) Who knows? Who fucking cares? I don't. (*He makes a pillow of his jacket.*) Wake me when the buzzer blows. I'm gonna have a little sleep, see if I can dream a way of getting over there to those little birdies—then by God you'll see some organ playing . . . yes, sir, there'll be some tonguing going down that's really in the groove . . . Uh, mmm.

(*Lights fade slowly to black at the end of Act One.*)

Act Two

Scene One

ANGELA *goes across to* JUDITH *to offer cup of coffee.)*

ANGELA: Coffee, Judith?

JUDITH: What? Oh, thank you . . . Kind of you . . .

ANGELA: I haven't touched it. (*Wipes nose on back of her hand.*) So it's all right. No bugs round it or anything. . . .

JUDITH: Look, I'm sorry about that . . . I . . .

ANGELA: Nah, you're right, I am a scruffy un everybody says. Me fiancé's always getting on to me for messing up his car and well . . . it's just me, isn't it . . . ?

JUDITH: (*About to sip coffee.*) Oh, but what about you?

ANGELA: I'll have mine after. S'all right. Go on. I can see you haven't brought anything with you.

JUDITH: Silly of me. I didn't know where the agency would send me but I thought I'd be near some shops or a cafe at least . . .

ANGELA: Nah, nothing round here. You have to go over the bridge, miles away. That's why this firm moved their main office into town because all the staff kicked up about there being no amenities . . . And besides it was dangerous on a winter's night, leaving here in the dark . . .

JUDITH: I'll bet.

ANGELA: Used to work for this firm. But I packed it in . . .

JUDITH: Mmmm . . . The coffee's very welcome . . .

ANGELA: Here, have a sarny . . .

JUDITH: No . . . I . . .

ANGELA: Go on. It's corn dog. Hope you don't mind onions.

JUDITH: Love onions.

ANGELA: For me cold. And if the two of us are eating onions we won't notice it when we breath over one another will we?

JUDITH: True.... I'm really in your debt (*For the sandwich*).

ANGELA: Think nothing of it. You're welcome. You'd do the same for me, wouldn't you?

JUDITH: Yes ... yes, I would ...

ANGELA: Well then. Fill yer boots ...

JUDITH: What?

ANGELA: There's plenty here. Me Ma always sees I'm well fed ... Here, come on, dig in yer at yer grannies ...

JUDITH: Thank you ...

ANGELA: Don't expect you look after yourself proper on your own.

JUDITH: I do all right.

ANGELA: Bet you don't. Bet you don't cook for yourself nor nothing. Bet you just go down the Chinese or you make do with a Big Mac ...

JUDITH: Well, this is true, on your own you ...

ANGELA: Hey, listen, I'm sorry for bringing that up ...

JUDITH: No. No. It's quite all right ...

ANGELA: No. I can be a real irritating bitch at times. I'm such a nosey bitch an' all.

(JUDITH *is forced to laugh, choking on sandwich at* ANGELA'S *seriousness.* ANGELA *pats her on the back.*)

ANGELA: Nah, it's true. My fiancé's always telling me, "You know what?" he says, "You're a right nosey little cow you are." An' he's right, I am. An' I'm sorry to pry . . .

JUDITH: It doesn't matter . . .

ANGELA: I always gets peoples' backs up then they stop speaking to me, an' I don't know what I've done. An' I couldn't stand working in here an' not speaking all day over. Not in this God-forsaken hole. I'd go crackers. But the trouble with me is I always speak before I think. I say what's in me head. One second it's in me head, next minute it's out. So you haven't got to take much notice of what I say. Nobody else does. I shall have to learn to do better . . .

JUDITH: I was too hasty. Too rude . . .

ANGELA: I should have known I'd upset you . . .

JUDITH: It touched a nerve I thought was dead, that's all . . .

ANGELA: Would do, some idiot saying a thing like that.

JUDITH: I was surprised to find it was still alive. And it shocked me.

ANGELA: It makes you think, though, dun it? I mean, I've been thinking a lot lately about how sad it all is . . .

JUDITH: Sad?

ANGELA: Breaking up . . .

JUDITH: It's the way it goes. . . .

ANGELA: Ah but, somebody you make a home with. All that waste when it goes wrong . . .

JUDITH: You can't expect too much . . .

ANGELA: No but it is sad, you got to admit . . .

JUDITH: We expect too much of each other. Our hopes are often beyond practicalities . . .

ANGELA: Yes, but the way blokes and women are these days. It isn't right, is it? I mean, it's not fun now, is it? All this watching you don't get owned by anybody. And if you break up who owns what and all that. All the joy's been taken out of it.

JUDITH: I don't suppose it was ever any different . . .

ANGELA: I'd like it the way it is in these telly series, you know, about the old days? Sounds daft I know, and I wouldn't say it to anybody else, but life would be nice like that. Costumes and wigs and people showing a bit of manners and politeness.

JUDITH: It covered a multitude of sins.

ANGELA: Nah, it was better like that. When a bloke came to court you and all that. Musta been nice. You know—he turns up with a box of chocolates with a string of pearls inside it . . .

JUDITH: That he's dived down to the bottom of the ocean for himself. Pickin' 'em with his teeth.

ANGELA: That's it. And he takes yer hand and kisses it. His tash tickles yer wrist. Now they're not satisfied unless their tash is ticklin' yer . . .

JUDITH: Quite.

ANGELA: Can't be healthy . . . Can it?

JUDITH: No . . . I . . .

ANGELA: Did your husband?

JUDITH: What?

ANGELA: You know want to . . .

JUDITH: Oh, as the mood took him.

ANGELA: And er . . . did . . . ?

JUDITH: We'll never get through all this work.

ANGELA: They get worked up, don't they?

JUDITH: Worked up?

ANGELA: Over boiling with the randies. Like that lot down there.

JUDITH: That's true.

ANGELA: But it soon cools off. When it's all over. It's 'Gi'e us a cuppa tea, darlin'!" and on goes *Match of the Day* or *Midweek Sports Special* on the telly and you become a back number out in the kitchen.

JUDITH: Why don't you send him out to make the tea?

ANGELA: He'd never make it through the door. He's too knackered, in he? I has to carry him.

JUDITH: You must be giving him something pretty powerful.

ANGELA: Nah, they just can't take it. They think they can. They do all this shouting and that but when it comes to it they soon peter out. Didn't you find?

JUDITH: I . . .

ANGELA: Or maybe you forgot . . . Oh, I'm sorry . . .

JUDITH: No matter.

ANGELA: Only it bothers me something shocking. You see, whatever you say about wanting to live your own life and all that you still want to be together with a bloke, don't you?

JUDITH: Well, with some other person, yes . . .

ANGELA: Well, I mean, yeah, I know, I get you. You might want to be with another bird or whatever I know, that's okay if that's for you. But for me it's blokes. But yet, no matter how you fancy a bloke or what you think about him you don't know how it's going to turn out.

JUDITH: That's the chance you take . . .

ANGELA: Yes, but you see, if you don't know how it's going to turn out, you don't know how much to put into it . . .

JUDITH: Sounds to me like you've already put quite a bit into it . . .

ANGELA: Well, Frank has, gotta admit. It's him who wants to get married . . . Ah, I get you, you were being funny . . .

JUDITH: A feeble attempt . . .

ANGELA: I can't explain what I mean correctly. You see, I was looking forward to getting married. I was always thinking about how it would be. Would it be nice like me mam and dad. Then I hear so much about break ups. All me friends have broke up . . . then there's the kids and . . . well, I . . .

JUDITH: You can't worry about that at the beginning. If you are that worried you shouldn't go through with it.

ANGELA: I know. But . . .

JUDITH: Though you go into it as wholeheartedly as you can, you learn to keep a little of yourself in the shade where it won't get burnt.

ANGELA: I don't think you understand my meaning.

JUDITH: I do.

ANGELA: Go on then.

JUDITH: You want to play. You like the fun. But you don't want to get hurt. You can't have it both ways.

ANGELA: But *you* must have been hurt.

JUDITH: Yes. I was.

ANGELA: I mean, look at you, I bet you don't sleep nights . . .

JUDITH: I was very hurt.

ANGELA: And you must have hated. You must have been full of hatred.

JUDITH: Yes. I have been. Perhaps I still am. But it's no use making that your life, is it?

ANGELA: Women always come off the worst.

JUDITH: Not always. We're all, men and women, in the same boat . . .

ANGELA: Women have feelings.

JUDITH: Everyone isn't the same. We all have our own

ACT TWO

needs. Anyway, come on, let's get some more work done.

ANGELA: Sorry for going on so much.

JUDITH: That's okay.

ANGELA: Only, it does worry me, see.

JUDITH: Yes. I understand.

(JUDITH, *not fully attentive, working, as* ANGELA *talks. As* ANGELA *talks she moves over to window now and then to look out.*)

ANGELA: When we knew we were going to get married, I couldn't think of anything else. Just Frank. The house. The way we were going to live. That's all I lived for. This last few months we've been making our preparations. That was all right. We got on okay. Now, our parents are starting to take over. For them it's like some big show they're putting on. They're all trying to outdo the other. They're living their big day all over again, through us. I realized the other day this wedding has got nothing to do with Frank and me. We're just puppets. We're getting married for them. So we can fit their world. You see, I took this job just for the extras we need. Now, I feel like taking the money I've earned over the last few weeks and buggering off. Anywhere, so nobody can find me. The wedding's only three weeks away.

JUDITH: It's natural to feel like you do at this stage.

ANGELA: I've started thinking about all that freedom slipping away.

JUDITH: Yes.

ANGELA: And I've never really had any freedom. I've always done what somebody else wanted me to do. Sometimes I think, "Stuff you! I'll do what I want. Just once. For a change."

JUDITH: Well, why don't you?

ANGELA: When I think I'll never go out with anyone else again. Seriously, I mean.

JUDITH: It's your choice.

ANGELA: Ah, but is it? That's what bothers me.

JUDITH: Then it's time you found out.

ANGELA: How?

JUDITH: Something may come along out of the blue and change you. Who knows? A lot can happen in three weeks.

ANGELA: Mum can't understand why I get so bad tempered these days. "You've got it made, lass," she says. "You don't know you're born. Back in my day . . ." And that makes me see red. I can't argue with her. I just have to act silly. I know I act silly. I see myself doing it. I can't stop. It's the only relief I get. I don't know what to do about it. When I try to tell anyone about it all they say is, "Oh, you're thick, you're stupid, you're not meant to think." Maybe they're right.

JUDITH: Never think that. Never let anyone stop you thinking for yourself . . .

ANGELA: Yes, but I don't understand myself because when I get married, I'll have everything. I'll never have to do a hand's turn. And my parents, they struggled. They had it rough. They had nothing when they married, I won't even need to go to work.

JUDITH: So what'll you do, stay home?

ANGELA: I don't want to, Not if I can find a proper job. I get bored with this temping lark, but at least it gets me out and it gets me meeting people like you. People I can talk to. I've never met many people I can talk to. Not round our way. Nobody like you, at any rate. I'll lose all that at home. I mean, Frank wants me to have kids right away. You know why?

JUDITH: I can guess.

ANGELA: So he's got me tied down from the word go.

JUDITH: Ah.

ACT TWO

ANGELA: Know what he said last night? He's going to fill me up with six.

JUDITH: Only six?

ANGELA: So, I'm stuck at home dependent on him.

JUDITH: Pity you couldn't fill him up with six, then he'd understand.

ANGELA: Yes, let him carry a bellyful of arms and legs around with him for nine months see how he likes it.

JUDITH: That's right.

ANGELA: Ah, but it's his reasons for wanting me to be stuck at home that worries me. I mean is he going to be off gallivanting? Finding other bits of stuff? Why's he want me stuck at home?

JUDITH: You could be taking him too seriously. They say these things. In the heat. You know.

ANGELA: No. You don't know him. He just wants to show his power. Sometimes he's like a reincarnation of what's that feller? Rudolph Hitler. He just has to be boss. King Kong. Why's it always like that?

JUDITH: It's the way we're made.

ANGELA: But why?

JUDITH: I wouldn't presume to know.

ANGELA: There's gotta be a reason.

JUDITH: I can't give you answers.

ANGELA: But you know more than me.

JUDITH: I wouldn't bank on that ...

ANGELA: You're educated.

JUDITH: Well ...

ANGELA: Somebody's got to have the answer.

JUDITH: Yes, when you're young you think there's someone somewhere knows what it's all about. Someone somewhere. Some Big Mammy, some Big Daddy, has got it all under control. But as you get older you find it isn't true. There really is no one in charge. And no one person knows enough to answer the questions that're beginning to bother you.

ANGELA: It's a poor do.

JUDITH: It's a battlefield.

ANGELA: Why should it be?

JUDITH: You have to accept it and hope it may change one day.

ANGELA: You're right, what you said. I do want all the fun and all the security of marriage, but not all the trouble, and the thought of belonging to someone all the time scares me . . .

JUDITH: You'll have to re-think it all.

ANGELA: I am thinking and that's what scares me most. Sometimes, I wish I could find some excuse. Anything I can use to get out of it . . .

JUDITH: Like I say. It's natural.

(*A buzzer sounds off (or clarion). Fade down lights on Stage One.*)

Scene Two

(*Lights up on Stage Two.*)

(*The men, still sunbathing.* JEFF *and* BAILEY *get to their feet, gather their things together, prepare to put their shirts back on.*)

BAILEY: (*Prodding the still-prone* JACKO *with his boot.*) Now then, Jacko . . .

JACKO: Yeah, yeah.

BAILEY: Gotta get back to earn your dollar.

ACT TWO

JACKO: Yeah, yeah. Roll on the day the eagle shits.

BAILEY: Whatsamatter, broke already?

JACKO: After playin' cards with you I should think so.

BAILEY: Ye'. You gotta go some to beat me.

JACKO: (*On his feet, smacking his lips.*) Christ, me mouth's as dry as a nun's crutch. Give us a sip of that beer, Bailey.

BAILEY: Not much left.

JACKO: Less see if I can squeeze some out ...

(*Takes flagon. Tips his head right back, then gives it back to* BAILEY, *who tips it to show it is empty, then drop kicks it away.* JEFF *is looking back across river at the house.* JACKO *glares belligerently at him.*)

JACKO: No good you looking over there.

JEFF: (*Turning away, shrugging, being flip.*) A cat can look at a queen can't it.

JACKO: Yes, but it ain't gonna do it much good, is it?

(*On Stage One,* ANGELA *is on spotlight again, looking seemingly unconcerned about the men out of the window, maybe miming chatter to* JUDITH (*who is still in the black*).)

BAILEY: There she is again.

JACKO: That's the young un.

BAILEY: Is it?

JACKO: Yes, you can see the ...

BAILEY: Ah, yeah. Now I see.

JACKO: In it lovely?

JEFF: (*About to move away. Looks back.*) Yes, I've got to admit.

BAILEY: (*As if strangely disapproving.*) She likes to show herself off that one.

JACKO: For Jacko.

BAILEY: Reckon so, do you?

JACKO: I can feel it between us from all the way over there. The vibes.

BAILEY: The balls.

(*He winks, and* JEFF *smirks.*)

JACKO: The vibes, Bailey, my son, the vibes. She's dying for Jacko. She wants me. I can feel it. I am the answer to her prayer.

BAILEY: (*Winking at* JEFF *again, indicating 'nutter.'*) Whooo—ooo. Who's for the loony hatch, then?

JACKO: Yes, she's dying for it all right. I know. I have knowledge of such matters.

(ANGELA, *in spotlight for the first time, looks right across at the men.*)

JACKO: See that! See that! I told you! Wheeeey eeeeey, darlin! Yer a little cracker . . . Wheeey eeeeey.

(JACKO, *waving his trilby dances forward to edge of stage, performing a weird sort of snake dance.*)

JACKO: Heeeey ay yeeey.

BAILEY: What's that supposed to do for her?

(ANGELA *watches* JACKO *curiously.*)

BAILEY: (*To* JEFF.) Look at this. Queen o' Sheba and the dance of the seven veils. Jacko, you nutter . . .

JEFF: What a Berk.

(JACKO *accompanies his performance with weird cooing noises, which astonish and amuse* BAILEY *even more and more. They also amuse* ANGELA. *Still in spotlight, she turns to look back into the office.*)

BAILEY: That's no way. She thinks you're a nut dancing around like that.

(JEFF *looks up at the sky with a gesture of contempt and despair, whilst at same time wondering if he ought to get in on the act.*)

ACT TWO

JACKO: You wait'll she turns round again. I'll really turn it on. I'll mesmerize her with me body. Trick I learned from a spade I worked with one time in a Wolverhampton scrap yard.

BAILEY: (*Embarrassed for* JACKO.) No. Look, you don't wanna caper round like that. Get yourself talked about.

JACKO: (*Looking over river: Hopefully.*) You wait.

BAILEY: Idiot. First class.

(ANGELA *looks down again.*)

JACKO: There, see! Here we go. Whhhheee Eeeeh.

(*He dances again more crazily than before. This time, with mouth organ clamped between his teeth, his dance becomes something of a feature. He struts, he capers, he does the splits. He rolls over. He gets up. Struts again—Mick Jagger mixed with Max Wall. He dances more and more lewdly, limbo style, until he's down on his back, thrusting up and out his groin.*)

BAILEY: Gerrup! Gerrup! You great daft twat. Gerrup.

(ANGELA *turns in spotlight and beckons* JUDITH. JUDITH, *invoices in hand, joins her in spot light.*)

BAILEY: Come on, Jacko, gerrup, you great screwball. Gerrup.

(*The girls remain in spotlight.*)

(JACKO, *on his back, rolls over, stares up and over, straining, begging for applause.*)

(ANGELA *laughs.*)

(JACKO *rises and bows to the girls. Doffs his trilby in a big sweep. Just when everybody thinks he's finished, as an encore he dances again, this time in Chaplinesque fashion.*)

(ANGELA *applauds.*)

JACKO: I've got her . . . Got you my lovely . . .

(JUDITH *takes* ANGELA *by the arm to lead her back to work. They move out of spotlight. Lights fade on Stage One.*)

(JEFF *stands with arms folded, stiff. He might have liked to join in with* JACKO, *but can't make himself do so.*)

JEFF: They've gone, Jacko.

BAILEY: (*Alongside* JACKO. *They both look up.*) Ye', they've gone.

JACKO: (*Making fist.*) We're all right here. That first little cracker (ANGELA) is mine. And is she going to be lucky! Did she know when she woke up this morning she was going to be so lucky? I'm gonna show her things she's only dreamed about. You'll have to make do with the other one, Bailey. Sorry and all that, but you'll be all right, won't you?

(JEFF *sniggers in contempt at* JACKO.)

BAILEY: Yes, I'll be all right. I'll be all right with the pair of them.

JACKO: Don't be greedy now, Bailey. Don't make yer eyes bigger'n yer whatsit.

BAILEY: No danger.

JACKO: Anyway, that little un is more in my line. And she can't wait for me.

(JEFF *is strolling around, picking up his things—book, etc.—whistling loudly, tunelessly, pointedly.* JACKO *is catching on, and turns away from looking across the river, to glare after* JEFF.)

JACKO: You know, I really hate that sarky melt.

(JEFF *whistles* "Colonel Bogey" *as he's about to stroll off.* JACKO *catches him by the arm.*)

JACKO: You know the trouble with you, Sonny Jim? You're just pissed you ain't getting a look in . . .

JEFF: (*Quickly shaking his arm free.*) Leave hold.

JACKO: (*Grabbing his arm again, looking ready to butt* JEFF.) I'll do you.

JEFF: (*Shrugging his arm away from* JACKO *again.*) Don't you know anything?

ACT TWO 67

JACKO: Hey, you wha'?

JEFF: Those birds over there aren't interested in you.

JACKO: They're not interested in you, that's what pisses you off, Sunshine.

JEFF: They're not interested in any of us. They're just . . . .

(ANGELA *is again at window, pretending to be picking something up.*)

JACKO: Look! She's letting me see her. She's giving me a view. And just look at her, Jeeeezus. I bet it's lovely. I bet I could. Woweeee. Mmmmmm. Mmmmmmmm.

JEFF: (*Deliberately riling* JACKO.) How do you know she's not giving *me* a view?

JACKO: (*Full of scorn.*) You?

JEFF: Me.

JACKO: You? (*He spits.*)

JEFF: What makes you think it's all for you? Why can't it be for me?

JACKO: Piss off! D'you hear this, Bailey? Piss off! You don't stand a chance. She's giving *me* the view, Boy. That's who she's giving the view to. Me. Jacko, Not you. You don't rate.

JEFF: What a clown you are, Jacko.

JACKO: I'm worried about you.

JEFF: (*Indicating the direction of the factory.*) We'd better get back into work.

JACKO: You know that, eh?

JEFF: We're late.

JACKO: I'm getting very worried indeed.

JEFF: You've no need to be.

JACKO: But I am. You hear?

JEFF: Forget it.

JACKO: You're like a Big Sheila.

JEFF: One day you'll find out . . .

JACKO: When?

JEFF: You'll see.

JACKO: How about now?

(JEFF *turns to* JACKO. *They look as if they're finally going to square up.* BAILEY, *showing a surprising, perhaps workmanlike neatness, has been tidying the lunchtime area—putting the piece of driftwood log and the packing case to one side, putting rubbish in a bag. He breaks in on* JACKO *and* JEFF.)

BAILEY: Come on, you two!

JACKO: (*To* JEFF.) What d'you say, eh?

JEFF: We're late.

JACKO: Stuff that. Let's find out what you are. Once and for all.

JEFF: Jacko. Give up.

JACKO: (*Obsessive.*) I'm worried about you. I can't rest 'til I've rooted you out. Til I know what you are.

JEFF: Don't let it bother you.

JACKO: It should bother you, the way you behave.

JEFF: Nothing to do with you.

JACKO: The way you go about. The way you walk.

JEFF: I walk the way I walk.

JACKO: Like a chick. Like a Sheila. With yer tight arse.

JEFF: I'm not going to tell you again, Jacko.

BAILEY: You two! I'm telling you!

JACKO: All I wanna know, Bailey. All I wanna establish with this guy is, do I fight him or do I fuck him.

JEFF: (*About to go for* JACKO, *then changing his mind, turning away.*) You're a waste of time.

JACKO: (*Goes after* JEFF, *detains him again.*) Lissen, a bit of advice . . .

ACT TWO 69

JEFF: I don't need any advice from you, Jacko.

JACKO: Sure you do. Lissen. You know why you don't score.

JEFF: How do you know whether I score or not?

JACKO: I know, man.

JEFF: You don't know anything I do, outside of work.

JACKO: (*Smiling.*) I know, man. I know. I have insight. I have special knowledge. I see your problem. I'm willing to bet you've never scored. A tenner to a pinch of shite you've never been there ...

JEFF: You don't know.

JACKO: Name me one chick you've pronged.

JEFF: Just because I don't go mouthing it around.

JACKO: No, man. You're too tense and broody to score.

JEFF: You're tense.

JACKO: I ain't broody.

JEFF: You know bugger all about me.

JACKO: You're a Sheila.

JEFF: You don't know.

JACKO: It's obvious. Everything points to it. I mean, you ain't interested in the crumpet over there like we are.

JEFF: Not your way. No. I don't go for your way.

JACKO: That's the way they like it.

JEFF: No. You're way off beam.

JACKO: They may pretend different, Matey, but that's the way it's preferred when the chips are down and the meat's on the table. Oh, Oh, I know ...

(JEFF *is about to reply when* JACKO, *looking back, sees* ANGELA *once more in spotlight. Still holding* JEFF's *arm,* JACKO *says:*)

JACKO: See. She just can't stop looking at me, can she?

JEFF: But she's not looking at you. She's working.

JACKO: She's letting me see her. Jeeze it's lovely.

BAILEY: (*Who, after tidying up, has strolled off toward the factory, returns.*) Hey, you two lazy fuckers, we've gorra get in there. The gaffer's doin' his nut . . .

JACKO: (*To* BAILEY.) Tell him to piss off. (*To* JEFF.) See Jeff. I ain't kidding.

JEFF: She's just doing her work.

JACKO: No. She's letting me see what she's got to give me.

JEFF: You're sick, Jacko.

JACKO: I can't expect you to understand . . . Jeeeze it's lovely.

BAILEY: Jeff.

JEFF: Okay.

BAILEY: (*Waving off to the boss.*) Ye' ye', we're coming. We'll be right there. Fella here got a touch of the sun. We'll be right there.

JACKO: (*Angry.*) Yeah, we're coming you fat, pissy-arsed bastard.

BAILEY: (*Quietly*) Okay. Take it easy. Cool it.

(JACKO *and* BAILEY *are about to move off.* JEFF, *tucking paper back book into back pocket of his jeans, is about to follow when he turns round slowly to look back.*)

(JUDITH *appears in spotlight on Stage One to take* ANGELA *by the arm once more, to lead her back to her desk.* ANGELA, *this time, shakes her off.* ANGELA *looks directly down on* JEFF. *These two hold the look.* JEFF *is shy at first, then he smiles, puts up his arm to wave to* ANGELA. JUDITH, *who has moved off a pace or two, urges* ANGELA *back to work again, then turns away.*)

(JEFF, *still staring across river, leaves his hand at shoulder height. But as* ANGELA *has half turned to say something to* JUDITH *he shrugs, turns away.*)

ACT TWO 71

(*But* ANGELA *turns back to window to smile and wave again.* JEFF *has got his back turned and doesn't see her. However,* JACKO, *in turning round to see what* JEFF *is doing, sees* ANGELA *waving and smiling. He takes it to be meant for him.*)

JACKO: Oooooooh whoooo (*Waves his trilby. Does a little dance.*) What did I tell you?

(JEFF *turns back.* ANGELA *waves again.*)

JACKO: All for Jacko.

JEFF: (*Showing his vulnerability more than at any other time.*) No. She waved at me!

JACKO: I'm all right here I tell you.

JEFF: But . . .

(*Then* ANGELA *goes the whole hog and smiles and waves flauntingly.*)

JACKO: There she is. My little cracker. Oh, yes, I'm all right here.

(ANGELA *is blowing kisses, doing a wiggle and pout, in corny fashion.*)

JACKO: Oh darlin', I'm all yours! Oh, Oh . . .

(*He's about to put his hands to his mouth to bawl out more messages when* ANGELA, *with a last bump and grind, moves out of spot. Light goes out on Stage One, leaving* JACKO *teetering about, hardly able to contain himself on edge of Stage Two.*)

(JEFF *looks saddened by the fact of* ANGELA's *performance. He sees that after all it wasn't meant only for him.*)

JACKO: God. Oh, God. If only I had me bike for tonight. If only I could . . . Good Creepers . . . Oh, Man, Wooooweee. I gotta get across there. I gotta catch her before . . . How the . . . Jeeze . . . Gotta get out early . . . Ooh . . . my . . .

(*He's practically slavvering with excitement and the frustration of thinking this prize might yet get away.*)

(JEFF, *peeved-angry with* ANGELA, *angry with himself for fall-*

ing for ANGELA's *trick, angry with the world for not being the place he wants it to be, moves off.* JACKO *once again stops him, this time in a much-more friendly fashion.*)

JACKO: Hey, Jeffo, my ol' frien'.

JEFF: (*Trying to break away.*) What now?

JACKO: Did you see that, Jeffo? Did you see what she did?

JEFF: Yes. I saw.

JACKO: Well, Kid?

JEFF: So?

JACKO: Well, whatdya reckon me and you's gonna do about it?

JEFF: Come on . . .

JACKO: No, no, Jeff, loosen up, son, you're as screwed up tight as a fish's ear. Loosen up, Kid.

(*He puts his arm around* JEFF, *cuddles him, talks calmly, almost seductively.*)

JACKO: No need to be so tight, Kid. You're amongst friends. That's what I'm trying to teach you. We're all friends here and friends share . . . Okay . . .

JEFF: Look . . .

JACKO: (*Smiling*) Eh?

JEFF: Okay.

JACKO: So what are we gonna do about these chicks over there who're waitin' to be hatched?

JEFF: I don't know.

JACKO: (*Stroking* JEFF.) Sure you do. We go over there. Right? Right?

JEFF: (*Uncertainly, despite himself giving in to* JACKO.) All she did was wave.

JACKO: All she did was wave?

ACT TWO 73

JEFF: That's right.

JACKO: You kidding me?

JEFF: All she did was . . .

JACKO: You look me right in the eye. You look ol' Jacko right in the eye an' you tell him, without blinkin' that you don't know what's goin' on here . . . Come on, Jeffo. I don't really wanna think bad of you. You do know don't you. . . . ? Yes, sure, eh?

JEFF: She was just . . .

JACKO: Look, she waved, she wiggled, she gave it all this. (*Does bump and grind up close to* JEFF.) And she gave it plenty o' this . . . Eh, Bailey?

BAILEY: Yes. But . . .

JACKO: Then when she waved, her blouse fell open. And did you see what she gave us a glim of? Woh woh weee. Eh, Bailey. Could you see?

BAILEY: They were real good scrumpers. Real ripe little apples I give you that . . .

JACKO: I kid you not.

BAILEY: Yep.

JACKO: And she's gonna give them ripe little rosy apples to me an' I'm gonna eat 'em down whole in one quick gobble . . . uh?

JEFF: (*Trying to move away again as* JACKO *touches him.*) Knock it off.

JACKO: She's gonna make me a present of her little sweet basket of fruit . . .

JEFF: (*angry*) Why don't you sodding well grow up, Jacko?

JACKO: I am grown up. Looka here (*Touching himself*). Is that grown up or ain't it. Could you be more grown up than that. Even ol' Bailey here couldn't match that. You say that ain't grown up . . . You want to make sure it's real?

(*He reaches out for* JEFF's *hand to place it on his own penis, But* JEFF *shakes his hand away.*)

JEFF: Sod off, Jacko.

JACKO: Will if you want me to but I prefer what's on offer over there, right now.

JEFF: Just piss off, you make me want to bloody vomit.

BAILEY: (*Putting his arm around* JEFF's *shoulder.*) Take it easy, I told you, take no notice. You gotta get used to this. Now Jacko, you knock it off. You've gone too far.

JACKO: (*Also going to* JEFF *as* BAILEY, *after giving* JEFF *a pat, moves away.*) Hey, Jeffo, Jeffo, my ol' mucker, my ol' chum, you're getting me all wrong. You think I'm tryin' to put it over on you and you're wrong. For Chrissakes, man, we worked together for a couple o' months now an' we're still no closer together. I mean that's wrong? I tried every way to be mates wit' you. I get the elbow. Now that isn't on. I mean, I help you with yer job. I showed you how to get more out of your machine. I show yer all the dodges and the best places to have a bit of a skive when we're on nights. I mean I put myself out for you. But what the hell do you do for me? It's no wonder I get chocka and mess you around when yer so standoffish. Do you understand?

JEFF: Yes, but . . .

JACKO: So let's just have a bit of comradeship between us, eh? Like it exists between me an' ol' Bailey? Right, Bailey?

BAILEY: He's right, Jeff. Like I keep telling you.

JACKO: You get it now, Jeff?

JEFF: Yes.

JACKO: You see what we're about?

JEFF: Yes.

JACKO: Great. Great . . .

BAILEY: Well un, Jeff.

ACT TWO

JACKO: Put it there, Pal. (*They slap hands.*) Okay, that's good, that's a relief after all this time.

BAILEY: You're okay, Jeff.

(JEFF *is embarrassed, shy.*)

JACKO: Look at him, Man. We'll have the poor ol' bastard crying.

BAILEY: Leave him then.

JEFF: It's all right.

JACKO: Sure?

JEFF: Yes.

JACKO: Great. Great. Okay . . . Here's what we do. Okay, Jeff? Listen, Kid. Five o' clock comes. No messing about. The hooter blows. We're out through the gates like bats out of hell. We zoom over the bridge. We get round there. An' we catches they little pigeons just as they'm about to fly the coot, uh? So, I mean. Let's start cleaning the machines down at twenty to five. No hanging about, eh? Bailey my friend?

BAILEY: (*Dubiously, but showing bravado.*) You're damn right we will.

JACKO: Dead on five. We're out through them gates like bears after honey, dead on five, over tha bridge in Jeff's car. Eh?

BAILEY: Right.

JACKO: You're on, Bailey?

BAILEY: Too true.

JEFF: Wait a minute . . .

JACKO: This is gonna be a night to . . . Yes, Jeff?

JEFF: In my car?

JACKO: Sure.

JEFF: Come on . . .

JACKO: What's wrong?

JEFF: I go the opposite way.

JACKO: You kidding me? Lissen to him. He's kidding me again.

JEFF: No.

(JACKO *grins. Shrugs, full of charm, goes over to* JEFF, *puts his arm round his shoulder, very affectionately again.*)

JACKO: Jeff, Jeff, Jeff. Tonight, Jeff, my friend, you, me, and Mr. Bailey here, we go over the bridge together. Okay? (*He turns and kisses tips of his fingers toward office window.*)

JEFF: You don't stand a chance.

JACKO: Look, Jeff, you needn't be afraid me an' Bailey's gonna leave you out.

BAILEY: No. We'll let you have yer touch. Fact I might let you go before me . . . Since it's your car . . .

JEFF: (*Laughing nervously.*) You're a couple of jerks . . .

JACKO: Ah, come on, Jeff.

JEFF: A right couple o' jerks . . .

JACKO: You're not gonna let yer pal, Jacko, down now, are yer. An' yer ol' mate, Bailey?

BAILEY: No, he won't let me down.

JACKO: So come on, Jeff. Wassa marrer with you?

JEFF: Nothing. Nothing's the matter . . .

JACKO: Good, Kid, eh, Bailey.

BAILEY: Too true.

(JACKO *gives* JEFF *a cuddle.* BAILEY *also puts his arm over* JEFF's *shoulder, so* JEFF's *practically staggering under the weight of them.*)

(*Voice of Gaffer shouting off stage:* "Hey, are you coming, or aren't you, you fucking shower?")

JACKO: Ye', we'll be coming all right . . . We'll be coming in streams.

ACT TWO 77

JEFF: Rivers.

(BAILEY *laughs.*)

JACKO: What's he say?

BAILEY: Rivers . . .

JACKO: That's the ticket, Jeff . . .

(*They all move off together.*)

JACKO: (*Bawling old army song.*)
Salome, Salome,
That's my girl Salome . . .

(*Fade down lights. On tape, roar of machinery, almost deafening in factory. Aloud: mad voice of gaffer:* "Get on wit' yer bleddy work you lousy shower o' lazy sodding whore's bastards.")

(*Cut sound quickly.*)

Scene Three

(*Lights up.*)

(*As the river bank material was cleared by* BAILEY *in previous scene, and as river bank will not be seen again, the whole stage is used as an office.*)

(*When lights come up fully it is obvious that there is an "atmosphere" in the office, largely created by* JUDITH. *She is annoyed at* ANGELA *because, after talking earlier as if she really wanted to learn something here, she is being as silly as ever, moreso in fact.* JUDITH *feels she's wasted her time talking to her and has betrayed her own self by talking candidly to her and she hasn't the brains to be taken so seriously. She feels embarrassed by* ANGELA, *not only for her sake but for* ANGELA's *sake.* ANGELA *feels the atmosphere but pretends to be oblivious to it at first. Perhaps she feels a bit guilty at acting so daft and, as she said earlier, she can't understand why she did it.*)

(JUDITH *is sitting at the desk. She's watching* ANGELA, *who is just turning away from the window.*)

ANGELA: They've gone into work now.

JUDITH: You want to be careful, you know.

ANGELA: Wha?

JUDITH: Encouraging them.

ANGELA: Nah, s'all right.

JUDITH: You're playing a dangerous game.

ANGELA: Nah, s'all right.

JUDITH: You're playing a dangerous game.

ANGELA: Nah, it's only a bit of fun.

JUDITH: You went a bit too far.

ANGELA: It's what they like i'n it?

JUDITH: Maybe, but we don't have to supply.

ANGELA: Come on, don't be a misery. It's only a bit of fun.

JUDITH: Well, let's hope they see it as such.

ANGELA: Only a game. Only idiots take anybody fooling about like that seriously. I mean all blokes like a bit of tit show and that. Even me ol' Dad he likes having a laugh at it and Mum don't mind. Some of you people take things too seriously.

JUDITH: The reason women don't get taken seriously enough is because some women act like you just did.

ANGELA: Wha?

JUDITH: You become a caricature not a . . .

ANGELA: Ah, get knotted with all that stuff. What are you on about? It's only a bit of fun. Don't you like a bit of fun?

JUDITH: I can assure you there's nothing I like better. When I'm sure of my company. I can let my hair down . . .

ANGELA: I 'spect you can.

JUDITH: I have the same feelings as you . . .

ACT TWO

ANGELA: I 'spect you do, on the quiet. I've met your type before. I know . . .

JUDITH: But . . .

ANGELA: Aw, come on, here, have a peppermint, take two or three, here, have half the packet. Cool you down . . .

JUDITH: (*Smoothed for the moment.*) You're quite impossible . . .

ANGELA: Here get yerlaughing tackle round that . . . Come on, no good us falling out again. Too nice a day for that. An', you know wha'. I think me cold's clearing up. Musta been talking to you before. Musta got rid of summat on me mind. Cos you know I think it's only some sort of allergy. I mean I've kept on getting things wrong with me over the last few weeks. Headaches, spots, see I got a spot still here on me belly. It's all the anxiety lately . . . (*She sucks on peppermint loudly, clears one piece out of her teeth.*) Good, these, aren't they. (*Shows piece of peppermint on her tongue.*)

JUDITH: Very nice . . . Shall we . . . Get on.

ANGELA: Clear yer breath of the onions. Don' wanna meet Frank wi' me breath stinkin' o' onions.

JUDITH: No. Are you ready for me to read out . . .

ANGELA: Hey, though, that was bleddy funny wan it? Them blokes. You got to admit. Bleddy . . . Hey, listen, I reckon if they coulda got across that river . . . If the work's buzzer hadn't sounded, they'da been storming the walls . . . That's why I did it then. I knew they couldn't do ought. I bet they're frothing over the machines now, eh?

(JUDITH *looks at* ANGELA *again, torn between irritation at her conceit and surprise at what appears to be her innocence.*)

JUDITH: Yes.

ANGELA: Wuz funny though, wan it, eh? Go on. Say it was funny.

JUDITH: Yes.

ANGELA: Mind, don't you go telling my fiancé if you see him. It was only a bit of fun.

JUDITH: Yes. I know.

ANGELA: Anyway, I'm only getting me own back in a way. For the way he is.

JUDITH: Do you feel like doing any work now?

ANGELA: Me? I never felt less like bleddy work in my life ... Oh, here, have some chewy ...

JUDITH: No, it's okay ... I ... Shall we ...

ANGELA: (*Putting a chew ball in her mouth.*) Bleddy work.

JUDITH: Just keep thinking it's all in a good cause.

ANGELA: Pardon?

JUDITH: The big day. The nuptuals.

ANGELA: Oh, ah.

JUDITH: You said you only took this job to save for the wedding extras.

ANGELA: Ah, that's right.

JUDITH: (*Picks up invoices as* ANGELA *seats herself at machine.*) Ninety-one pounds ... (*She looks across at* ANGELA *and sees she's not concentrating, she's examining some spot on her leg.*)

ANGELA: (*Holding leg out.*) Not bad, eh?

JUDITH: I've seen worse.

ANGELA: Ah, me best feature. I do these exercises. But when I got that rash, it worried me. Had to wear black stockings all the time. Haven't got all that much summer clobber to go with black ...

JUDITH: Ninety-one pounds. ...

(ANGELA *blows out a bubble.* JUDITH *stands up and pointedly turns adding machine her way, begins to use machine. She works quietly on her own, trying to shut off* ANGELA, *as if she's given up on her. But, as she's like some big, daft, affectionate puppy, she can't shut her off altogether. She answers her, mainly dis-*

ACT TWO 81

tractedly, and sometimes with irony as she works. ANGELA *leans with her elbows on desk, looking across at her chewing gum, and now and again blowing out bubbles.*)

ANGELA: We're going out to that big carpet mill tonight. Frank's picking me up here dead on five. We're going to shoot over to the Mill and buy this gorgeous carpet. For the living room. Gorgeous. You see, we bought this super incredible painting on Saturday. Really nice . . .

JUDITH: Who by?

ANGELA: Wha'?

JUDITH: Who painted it?

ANGELA: Oh, I dunno, it doesn't matter.

JUDITH: It might to the artist.

ANGELA: Oh, I dunno, I forget such things. Though I used to know. I got me A-levels for art at school . . .

JUDITH: Did you?

ANGELA: Yeah, easy. That's why I'm good at picking pictures now. And this one's lovely. All in autumn colors. Just like a photograph. Frank didn't like it. Said it was rubbish. But I said, "Look how it goes with the carpet." Then he saw what I meant. Trouble with Frank, he ain't artistic, like. Thinks all that's woman's stuff. Anyway, he's all for it now. He's always staring at it and imagining things. He says he sees us strolling through the woods. Rolling about on the dead leaves. So, anyway, we're going to get this carpet tonight . . .

JUDITH: To roll about on?

ANGELA: Eh, yeah. That's it. Roll about. But Mum she put her foot in it. She says we shouldn't have it in the living room, under the picture. She says it's better in the sitting room. (*Pause as* JUDITH *counts under her breath the figures: "Ten-pounds thirty-six, sixty-six pounds sixty-nine . . ."* ANGELA *blows a bubble.*) But me and Frank want it in the living room, with the painting over the mantelpiece looking down . . . Then Frank's mother had to have her twopence worth. She says we ought to have it upstairs in the master bedroom. Where would you have it, Jude?

JUDITH: Pardon. Sorry?

ANGELA: Frank's mother says we should have it upstairs.

JUDITH: Well . . . well . . . it is conventional to . . .

ANGELA: Frank says he isn't going to let his mother dictate to us where we have it.

JUDITH: I should think not.

ANGELA: But then she did buy us this bedroom suite. And they're giving us this beautiful divan for the guest room. So she wants us to have it in the bedroom. Got to admit she's been good to Frank.

JUDITH: Well, have it in the bedroom, love.

ANGELA: But my mum and dad have been super, too. They've given us this lovely Chesterfield sofa and matching chairs . . .

JUDITH: And where do they want you to have it?

ANGELA: Like I said, Mum says it should be in the sitting room.

JUDITH: Well have it in the bedroom when your mother-in-law's around and . . . in the sitting room when . . .

ANGELA: Oh that would be a lot of messing around. I like to have things settled in one place.

JUDITH: Then you have it where *you* like.

ANGELA: Yes, we will in the end. (*Pause. She gets fed up of gum, discards it.*) Granny's been good too.

JUDITH: And where does she say you should have it?

ANGELA: Oh, she don't care so long as we get on and enjoy ourselves . . .

JUDITH: Very wise.

ANGELA: She is. She's great. She's given us this super

fantabulous incredible dresser. Must be over two hundred years old. And a lovely grandfather clock. The chime's gone but we can have that fixed. But we don't know where to put them. We're chocka block with furniture. Probably we'll store 'em for now in the back bedroom, out of the way. Everyone's been so sweet it isn't true. So I don't know what I'm complaining about. I mean we've got this smashing house, too. You should see it, Jude. Maybe you know where I'm talking about . . .

JUDITH: Where you'll be living?

ANGELA: Ye' . . . You know that Georgian Estate?

JUDITH: Georgian?

ANGELA: Ye', well some of the houses are Georgian. Some of 'em are pretty tasteless . . . We've got one of the Georgian ones . . .

JUDITH: (*Interested*) You've got a genuine Georgian house right slap bang in the middle of a new estate? An old house?

ANGELA: Nah, no. Not one o' them real old ones. Not for me and Frank. No. They only finished building our house last week. You know, up on the old railway line, that new estate. Georgian Homes Ltd., with the imitation gas lamps outside each door. You can imagine yer back in the days of coach and horses. They're painted black at the moment, the lamp standards. But Frank says he's gonna do' 'em over in red and white stripes. Cheer the place up a bit. I didn't want the house at first. Didn't like all them little winders. I like big ones (*Indicating windows of this office, which was once a fine old house.*). But Frank's dad gave us the deposit to put down and his uncle's firm built the houses. So I suppose we had to think ouselves lucky. Can't have everything you want, can yer? We'll live there for a while at least. Just to get started. Until Frank gets fully established in his partnership. He's a lawyer. Used to be in a bank. Now he's a lawyer. He's done well. (*She whispers.*) He's in the (*She waggles her fingers over her head, putting thumbs in her ears.*), you know . . . The Elks . . . and the Rotary Club . . . and . . . er don't say ought—the Masons. Should see him in his pinny with his pants leg rolled up. A scream. I suppose you have to laugh . . .

JUDITH: Ninety-five pounds six . . .

ANGELA: But he keeps his feet on the ground. He still likes to go out with the lads and go to footer . . .

JUDITH: Ten pounds only . . . Fifteen pounds . . .

ANGELA: I wouldn't want anybody who was soft . . . but I . . . Oh . . . I don't know . . . (*She watches* JUDITH. *And it slowly begins to dawn on her that perhaps she ought to be helping* JUDITH. *Then she forgets. Puts it out of mind.*)

ANGELA: I suppose really I'm lucky. Taken all round. I mean when you see these poor people on the telly, way they live. And all these people on the dole up and down, you know these poor sort o' workin' class people. You feel sorry. Frank says it's their own fault for bein' idle. They ought to get up and go, move around. But I dunno. It's all right for him. He's only ever lived at home. My dad knows what it was like years ago. And he told me. That's why he's kind now. You have to be glad people are so kind I suppose, but I don't know. I wish I could see something more of life. I mean, I'd like to see things differently to Frank. But I don't know where to look. And he's the only one I talk to. Not that he wants to talk much. He thinks I know nothing. Wants to keep it that way. (*Pause*) Hey, listen, I mean, you must come out and see us . . . Hey, Jude . . ?

JUDITH: Yes, yes. That would be very nice.

ANGELA: (*Looking toward window, singing absently.*)
Hey, Jude,
Don't wear a frown,
Take a sad song
And make it better.
Don't let it get under your skin . . .

ACT TWO 85

(*She has a pleasant voice. Again it makes* JUDITH *look up.* ANGELA *smiles.* JUDITH, *resigned, smiles back.*)

ANGELA: Hey, listen. Hey. Look, you come and see us. Frank will always pick you up and run you back.

JUDITH: That'll be very kind of him.

ANGELA: We'll be able to talk then . . . Hey, Ju . . . ude . . . don't be a fool. . . . Never remember the words of songs . . . but they had some good songs in the olden days didn't they . . . The Beatles and all that . . . Must have been great then . . . You know I cried when John Lennon got shot . . . Straight up. Cried all night . . . There's nobody like the Beatles now . . . Dire Straits, I don't mind them . . . (*Pause*) Bowie . . . Yes . . . (*Pause*) Hey, listen, did you have your own house?

JUDITH: What? Oh . . . house? Oh, yes. Yes.

ANGELA: Bet it was nice. You'd have a nice house I know. You being what you are. I'll bet it was nice.

JUDITH: Yes. It was. Nice.

ANGELA: I'll bet it was. You'd know what you wanted.

JUDITH: (*Looking up, showing bitterness.*) Yes. It was very nice. We lived in a *nice* district. Everyone had a nice garden, with regulation trimmed hedges and borders. Everyone had *nice* children. All had the correct jogging apparel, squash rackets, yellow wellies, thoroughbred dogs, all very *nice* and liberally proper we were, with all the right opinions from the right newspapers and satirical journals. All nice up-to-date young . . . ish couples. All in nice acceptable professions. Earning a decent thou, per year, with one or two nice real old honest, laborers around us we made sure we treated as equals. Even a friendly neighborhood tramp we left crusts out for. . . .

ANGELA: Ah, it's nice like that . . .

JUDITH: Yes. It is. We all got on so swingingly. (*Then she is ashamed of allowing her sarcasm to take over and to allow* ANGELA *to misunderstand her.*) Yes, well, it seemed nice at the time. It's what I thought I wanted. (*She begins to mark off invoices again.*)

ANGELA: Are you going to stay working as a temp?

JUDITH: Until I see which way the wind is blowing.

ANGELA: Won't you go back to the University?

JUDITH: Me? Not likely. I've had enough of that hypocritical racket. It's too full of bullshit for me. I always used to yearn to be at University once. That was my guiding aim. When I worked in other jobs I only had in mind I wanted to get into education. I worked my way up to it, studying in evenings. When I first left school at fifteen I worked behind the counter at Woollies . . .

ANGELA: So did I. Saturday mornings. After school.

JUDITH: Yes, well I did it because there was no other job for me. When I finished there I worked on a machine at a biscuit factory. My folks needed my money.

ANGELA: I wouldn't have guessed . . .

JUDITH: Yes, you would, if you knew where to find the joins . . . I studied my brains out. I thought education was the answer to everything. I thought remove the money factor from people's lives and it would all be different. It isn't. There's something more insidious. Power. And you find all the power-seeking pillocks like my ex-husband in education. You'd think they'd know better, but they don't. I'm sorry. You've got me on a bad day.

ANGELA: S'all right. I know what it's like. The first day is always worst for me. Pain is chronic . . . I have to have brandy . . . They might ask you to stay on with this firm at the head office. You seem to know what you're doing. I could put a word in for you.

JUDITH: That's good of you.

ANGELA: My auntie's a supervisor. Accounts. Would you like me to have a word?

ACT TWO

JUDITH: Actually I might move on elsewhere.

ANGELA: Move away? Don't you like it round here?

JUDITH: It's all right. But there are too many ghosts. And it isn't my place . . . I . . .

ANGELA: Didn't think you came from round here. Where would you move to?

JUDITH: Oh, I don't know. I really don't know. I expect I shall just stick a pin in the map.

ANGELA: You're used to moving round?

JUDITH: I'm no stranger to it. I've got out of the way of it recently but I expect I'd soon get back to how I once was . . .

ANGELA: I'd like to do that. Just take off.

JUDITH: Yes.

(*She looks at invoices again. She's about to use machine again. Then* ANGELA *turns adding machine so that the keys face her.*)

ANGELA: Here, come on, let me do that. That's my job.

JUDITH: Okay. If you're sure you're ready now.

ANGELA: Ye'. Ye'. Course I'm ready. Can't let you do all the work by yourself, can I? What do you think I am . . . Read 'em out . . .

JUDITH: You're ready?

ANGELA: Ye'. Ye'. Ready. Carry on.

JUDITH: Twenty-five pounds twenty.

ANGELA: Roll on five o' clock . . . Twenty-five pounds twenny . . .

JUDITH: Firty-fix times firty-free . . .

ANGELA: Flirty-flix slimes flirty-flea. Right.

JUDITH: Farty-sax pahnds nahnty-fahve.

ANGELA: Fatty-sex pooonds nointy-foive.

JUDITH: Ten pounds fifteen.

ANGELA: Ten pounds fifteen . . .

(*Slowly fade out lights as their voices drone on. Then bring up slowly again as a light change to denote the passing of the afternoon.*)

(*The buzzer or clarion sounds from across the river.* ANGELA *is making a complete total on machine. Both she and* JUDITH *look tired, weary, sweaty.* JUDITH *has unloosed the top of her skirt for more comfort, she wipes down around her throat with a tissue and the backs of her knees.*)

ANGELA: (*Wearily*) Four hundred and fifty-five thousand and seventy-nine pence . . . (*She checks another list.*) Thank Christ for that.

(*She tears off adding list and passes it to* JUDITH, *who pins it to a batch of invoices. She ties them together with an elastic band. She looks around at all the other batches of invoices around the office. (Perhaps a few piles have been added during light change).* ANGELA *also looks around. Both are too tired to take any pleasure in the work completed.*)

JUDITH: Looks like we finished them all.

ANGELA: Yes. It's all finished.

(JUDITH *goes to begin packing invoices into cardboard boxes tidily.* ANGELA *sniffs at her armpits.*)

ANGELA: Crikey, I pong like an old polecat . . .

(*She takes out a stick of roll-on deodorant from her bag and pushes nozzle down inside armpit of her blouse, rubs it around. Also down between her breasts, etc.* JUDITH, *meanwhile, continues to finish tidying up.*)

JUDITH: I suppose they'll send one of their vans out here in the morning to pick them up.

ANGELA: I s'pose so . . .

JUDITH: So we won't be coming back here.

ANGELA: Thank God.

JUDITH: What do we do, check with the office in the morning see where our next assignment is?

ANGELA: That's right. Don't forget to fill yer time sheet in. And remember to put down we worked through lunch (*She takes out her lipstick.*). It would be great if we got a job somewhere together tomorrow. But I don't suppose we will. I think I've got to go up to the zoo, on the turnstiles. That won't be so bad. I can go and have a look at the animals in the break. I'll love that. Hey, Jude, we might get together again, but if not, you know, all the best and that. It's been smashing working with you.

JUDITH: Yes. Thank you. I hope everything works out for you.

ANGELA: Oh, I s'pect it will . . .

JUDITH: Hope you get the carpet laid in the right place.

ANGELA: You'll have to come up and see us. Don't forget. We've had a laugh, though, haven't we, eh?

JUDITH: Yes.

ANGELA: All them crazy blokes out there. Gawd, laugh!

(*It's obvious that now the job is over, the thing that brought them together, communication between them is also at an end, or at least it would be very difficult for them to maintain. They have so little in common.* JUDITH *is listening to a sound from outside.*)

ANGELA: What's up?

JUDITH: Listen . . . I thought I heard a car stop outside.

ANGELA: Didn't hear nothing.

JUDITH: Could be your Frank. (*She goes to window, tries to see down.*)

ANGELA: Is it a Porsche with a pewter finish?

JUDITH: Can't see anything from here. Whoever it is must have parked round the back.

ANGELA: (*Her face isn't right yet, so she can't go to the window.*) Can't be anybody. You'd have heard the engine, and if it was Frank he'd have sounded his horn. There'd be no mistaking Frank.

JUDITH: Perhaps you'd better go down and see. If it is your fiancé you go on. I'll lock up here and phone into the firm on the way home ...

ANGELA: (*Now intent on her eyelashes.*) No, let him come up.

JUDITH: Thought you were in a hurry to get off to see to this carpet.

ANGELA: Wha'? Oh, ye', I suppose so. What are you doing tonight? Something exciting I suppose. It's such a nice night. Be great to do something exciting ...

JUDITH: Oh, yes. Very.

ANGELA: Oh. What?

JUDITH: Well, if no one else in the house I'm existing in at present has the same idea, I'm going to put about five pounds in the bathroom meter, take a radio and a book in there and have a good long soak. And I look forward to that very much indeed.

ANGELA: Oh. Oh. Yes.

(*Never having lived in a flat and shared a communal bathroom, ANGELA does not understand that this is a real luxury to be looked forward to.*)

(JUDITH *has by now filled the boxes,* ANGELA *is having a last look at herself in the mirror of the compact and is about to slide off the desk where she is perched when* JACKO *enters the office from the stairs. He is followed by* BAILEY, *who has his haversack over his shoulder and his cap and coat on now.* JEFF *comes into the office and stands by the door.*)

(ANGELA *sees them in the compact mirror. She is too shocked to move. Their attitudes to her are menacing, though* JACKO *is smiling and* BAILEY *and* JEFF *look not altogether comfortable.* JUDITH, *her back to door, feels their presence rather than hears them, and turns. The first person she has eye contact with is* JEFF, *who looks away quickly, then tries to look back more boldly. Then she looks at the solid, deadpan* BAILEY, *and she starts as if she recognizes him but isn't sure. Then she looks at the grinning* JACKO, *who tips his trilby.* ANGELA *slowly drops compact in her bag and turns to face* JACKO. JACKO *sees the astonishment on* ANGELA's *face. Now he is close up to her. He tilts his trilby to an angle, pushes his hand up to shoulder height, wiggles his fingers, trying for a boyish, charm: Hi!*)

(ANGELA *looks over to* JUDITH—"*Oh lor!*"—*appealing for help.*)

(JUDITH *stays quiet. She wants the men to make the first move so that she can react.*)

ANGELA: (*Trying for a haughty manner, perhaps in imitation of what she believes* JUDITH *would say.*) I'm afraid we're closed.

(JACKO *looks right into* ANGELA's *eyes, then suddenly chuckles loudly. Then he looks over at* BAILEY, *who shuffles around embarrassed, as if ready to turn round and go out. He forces a grin.*)

JUDITH: (*In her best deb manner.*) Yes, I'm afraid we're just about to lock up.

(JACKO *cackles.*)

JACKO: No need for you to be afraid, love, either of you.

JUDITH: Well . . .

JACKO: (*Smiling a bit more charmingly.*) You see, it's like this. I knew you'd be ready for knocking off about now. Said so, didn't I, Bailey? I said those two ladies will be ready to be away around five. That's what I said, din I Bailey?

BAILEY: (*Giggling a little with nerves, and at* JACKO's *far-fetched manner.*) Yes, that's right.

JACKO: So, I said, those two little birdies must be sweltering in that old house over there. Why don't we close down our machines early, never mind all the bonus, get across there and take them for a drink, a little beejoo drinkiepoo, eh?

JUDITH: (*With a smile.*) Well. We appreciate the thought . . .

JACKO: Do you? Good. That's great. What did I tell you, Bailey?

JUDITH: But ...

JACKO: Yes?

ANGELA: We don't know you.

JUDITH: And ...

JACKO: Say no more. Soon put that right. (*He points to his chest.*) Me. Jacko. Me. (*Points to the still-grinning BAILEY.*) My good friend, Bailey ...

JUDITH: Yes, I know ... You came to do the garden at my old house ... (BAILEY *shuffles uncomfortably, looks as if he'd like to take off.*)

JACKO: There you are you see. Small world, i'n it? Know each other already ... Oh, and that's the guy who has the car. (*He indicates* JEFF *with his thumb.*)

JUDITH: It's a very pleasant thought and thank you very much ...

JACKO: So how about it, love? (*He smiles charmingly at* ANGELA.)

JUDITH: But her fiancé will be here any minute ...

ANGELA: And we don't really know you ...

JACKO: (*Holding out his hand to* ANGELA.) You'll soon get to know me. (*Quietly*) Come on, love, let's go. You know it's right ...

JUDITH: You do see, don't you?

JACKO: I was talking my little lady here, love, if you don't mind. Let her speak for herself. She can speak to her Jacko. (*Quietly. Seductively.*) Now then, love, what's your name?

JUDITH: Her fiancé will be here any minute.

JACKO: (*Without turning*) Please.

ANGELA: Yes. Frank will be here. (*She aimlessly holds out her finger with engagement ring on it.*) You see?

ACT TWO

JACKO: Yes. So?

(*He turns to look at* BAILEY, *who laughs at* JACKO's *expression.*)

ANGELA: Well, you see.

JACKO: We ... ll. I don't see. I don't understand. What's the problem?

JUDITH: It's going to be awkward if Frank finds you here.

JACKO: I must be thick. I mean, who's it going to be awkward for?

JUDITH: Angela.

JACKO: Angela! What a lovely name. I always dreamed I'd meet an angel called Angela. Angela ... Angel ... Ah ... Now, Angela, just why is it going to be awkward, Angela, mine?

ANGELA: It is. That's all. It's going to be very awkward.

(JACKO *scratches himself, shoves his hand in his back pocket, sways around, suddenly looks boyishly gormless and inane. After a pause, swivels his head round to look at* BAILEY.)

JACKO: Perhaps you can help here, Bailey. As an experienced man of the world, will you kindly interpret this please? I don't understand it at all.

(BAILEY *shuffles around, shrugs at* JUDITH, *a bit apologetic.* JACKO *suddenly switches from being boyish and bewildered to harsh and sharp, a hint of what is to come.*)

JACKO: Well, well, speak out!

BAILEY: (*Chuckling*) Well, ...

JACKO: Yes?

BAILEY: Well, I think she's worried that er ... Frank?

JACKO: This Frank, yes, go on.

BAILEY: Frank will ...

JACKO: (*Snapping his fingers*) Got you. (*To* JUDITH) You

mean to say that this Frank will object to Angela coming for a drink ...

JUDITH: Yes. That's it. You've got it.

JACKO: With friends?

JUDITH: You could hardly be called friends.

JACKO: Eh?

JUDITH: Could you?

JACKO: After this afternoon? Jesus, Bailey, did you hear that?

(BAILEY *shrugs. Nods. Shakes his head.*)

JACKO: We could hardly be called friends, she says. What do you make of that?

BAILEY: I don't know, Jacko. Beats me.

(JUDITH *looks exasperated.*)

JUDITH: Oh, for heaven's sake ...

(*She's fed up with* JACKO *acting the fool, and the ridiculous situation she's been placed in.* BAILEY *winks at her, waves his hands—cool down.*)

(*Down,* JACKO'S *just a bit of a case.* JACKO *is now moving around, as if trying to solve this most complex problem.*)

JACKO: I mean, I don't understand. We could hardly be called. ... For Chrissakes we've all seen more of each other today than many friends see in a lifetime, eh Bailey ...

BAILEY: (*Remembering. Flushing. Looking a bit niggled at the idea of being laughed at by these women.*) Ye'. Ye. Too true.

JACKO: Don't tell me we're not friends after that. After what you've seen of us and ... Well, I dunno ... Isn't that right, Bailey.

BAILEY: (*Morose.*) I don't know. I can't answer.

(BAILEY *darts a glance at* JACKO, *knowing the edge is beginning to sharpen in him. He doesn't know yet what he'll do about*

ACT TWO

it. He loosens the haversack, ready to put down. JACKO *suddenly swivels round and looks at* JEFF.)

JACKO: You're a clever bugger. You sort us out here.

JEFF: You're absurd, Jacko. This is crazy. I knew it would be. Why don't you . . .

JACKO: Tcha! (*He waves contemptuously to shut* JEFF *off.*) Be quiet Professor . . . (*Then he tips his hat again to* ANGELA.) All right. Okay. I can catch the drift. Though I don't believe it in this day and age . . . But if this Frank is going to be a bit uptight. Right? About us being here, and about you coming with us for a drink, then let's blow before he shows.

ANGELA: (*Quietly, almost fascinated by* JACKO, *like a rabbit in front of a ferret.*) He's going to pick me up here, any minute, and . . .

JACKO: So you keep saying. But somehow I'm beginning to doubt it. I mean, why isn't he here before now? When did he say he'd be here?

ANGELA: Five o'clock. Dead on.

(JACKO *shrugs. Looks around. Looks very disappointed for* ANGELA's *sake.*)

JACKO: Hate to say this, but where the hell is he? It's long gone five.

(*He shrugs expansively, throwing his arms out. Then stopping, dropping his arms, moving over to* ANGELA, *he gently slips his arm around her waist.*)

JACKO: Now look here, Angie, I'm speaking to you as a friend. Don't you worry none about this Frank.

(ANGELA *tries to wriggle free, but* JACKO *digs points of his fingers into her ribs, at a point where it almost paralyzes her. Then she is forced to thrust against him. Then he lets her be.*)

JACKO: Jesus. Angie. You don't want to turn down the opportunity of an evening's fun for the sake of a man who doesn't even care enough to turn up on time. Christ, Angela, you're wasted on Frank. I mean. It makes my blood boil to see anybody treat a bird who looks like you, Angela, like the way Frank is treating you. You're too good for that. Anyway, don't fret. I think we can more than measure up to Frankie Fiancé when it comes down to giving some girls a bit of fun, that I can promise you . . .

JUDITH: But I don't reckon you can measure up to a Georgian home with a tall gas lamp outside.

JACKO: That's too deep for me.

JUDITH: Yes. It is. You're way out of your depth.

(JACKO *grins at* JUDITH. *Leaving* ANGELA's *side he does a "stroll" around* JUDITH, *looking her up and down as though examining a side of beef. Then he stops and looks right into her eyes.*)

JACKO: You know, me and you, we're not on the same wavelength as me and this one is. Pity because I believe I could really give you what you need. I'm sure I could open you up a little way. Let you see inside your self, let you see what's eating you. But the vibes between me and you are . . . (*He shakes his hand, then turns down his thumb.*) You know what I mean?

JUDITH: Oh, yes, completely. And I agree with you.

JACKO: It's as well to be straight isn't it?

JUDITH: Come on, Angela. We'll wait outside.

(JACKO *moves in quickly, blocking* ANGELA.)

JACKO: No. Wait. Just hang about. Do you really mean to tell me that you really don't want to come and have fun with us?

JUDITH: That's right. Now. . . .

JACKO: I'm talking to Angie. Angie is for me. You are for Bailey. Bailey will see to you. Maybe you underpaid for the gardening. Maybe you should give him a daisy chain at least. See to her Bailey. Shut her up.

(BAILEY *looks embarrassed. He tries for a "Well, you'll be all right with me" grin which is cowed when* JUDITH *glares at him haughtily, putting him down.*)

JUDITH: Don't you dare.

JACKO: Now then, Angela, my angel, you do want to have some fun with me, don't you?

(*He takes* ANGELA's *wrist. He pulls it up to his mouth, kisses it, licks the veins on the inside of her wrist.*)

JACKO: Because, I mean if not what were all those signals today, eh?

(*He pulls her close to him.* ANGELA *is flustered by this hard physical contact. She wrinkles her nose at* JACKO's *sweaty smell, while he revels in her aroma.*)

JACKO: Eh, Angie, eh?

ANGELA: I don't know what you're talking about.

JACKO: All that peekaboo and flashing.

ANGELA: Flashing?

(*He pulls back her blouse with his little finger and peeps down inside.*)

JACKO: Peepo. (*Lets blouse fall back into place.*) Yes. All that waving and come on.

(*He pushes himself close to her. Stares right into her eyes.*)

JACKO: Look into my eyes and face the truth, darlin'. It's all you can do. I'm the man who brings you the truth. And I'm loaded with good news.

(*There is a long pause. All the others are quite mesmerized by this performance.*)

JUDITH: Come on. Let's go.

JACKO: Will you shut up and keep out of it. (*He stares directly into* ANGELA's *eyes again, keeping her there, smiling.*) You were hiding here behind the window. You were watching us down there. You saw us. You know. Remember what you saw. Must have excited you more'n a bit. Come on now, admit it. No harm in admitting it. I mean, Christ, you must have seen a bit, you know. And you must have liked what you saw. Because you definitely started giving me the old come on. You liked me dancing for you, didn't you? I mean, I danced just for you, Angie . . . Now . . . what are you gonna do for little ol' Jacko . . . ?

JEFF: (*Breaking the spell.*) Jacko, you're pathetic.

JUDITH: Yes.

JACKO: That's just a voice from the dead. Ignore it.

ANGELA: Just let me by, please.

JUDITH: Yes. That's enough.

ANGELA: Please.

JACKO: Oh, don't listen to her. We haven't even got started yet and she wants to call it off. She's just jealous because she ain't gonna get what you're going to have . . . I mean if I had time I'd sort her out, put her straight, but you come first, Angie . . .

JUDITH: Look. Stop this damned foolishness this instant.

JACKO: Will you bloody shut up?

JUDITH: You've had your fun.

JACKO: We haven't that's just it.

JUDITH: This is as far as we're going.

JACKO: Christ, you're a real frigid mean-spirited old bitch, aren't you? No wonder you're such a miserable leftover-looking cow. I keep talking to Angie, you keep butting in. See to her, Bailey. Keep your woman in order, can't you? Now then, Angie, it's just me and you, girl.

ANGELA: Look, it was only a joke. If you can't take a joke.

JACKO: A joke, was it? I see.

ANGELA: That's all. We saw you down there before. It seemed funny.

JACKO: Seemed funny, eh?

ANGELA: Then you saw us, you started shouting and dancing and acting daft, so we, well I did, not Judith, just had you on. It wasn't serious.

JACKO: Not serious, Angie?

ANGELA: No, we were only joking.

(JACKO *looks over at* BAILEY.)

JACKO: Only joking they were, Bailey. What do you make of it? After all that, they were only joking.

BAILEY: I dunno.

(JACKO *stares at* ANGELA *then moves away from her. He stares at* JUDITH, *tips his hat over his eyes, pushes it back, looks at* ANGELA, *posed with his legs straddled, an inane look on his face.*)

JACKO: Only joking they were after all that.

JUDITH: (*To* BAILEY) I think your friend has been seeing too many old movies. Who does he think he is, a reincarnation of James Dean?

BAILEY: (*Laughs quickly*) That's it.

JACKO: What was that you said, bitch?

(JACKO *looks as if he might attack* JUDITH, *she stands her ground, facing him. He looks right into her eyes. He says slowly, quietly, almost in a whisper:*)

JACKO: Mean, humorless, hard done too, frigid, spunkless, bitch, as barren as a frosty cinder patch ... Right?

(JUDITH *continues to hold his gaze.*)

JEFF: Walk past him. He won't stop you.

JACKO: (*Turning from* JUDITH *to* JEFF.) Look, Sonny Jim, what is it with you? I invite you on a party and you turn into a right party pooper.

JEFF: Told you before, you're a clown, Jacko.

JACKO: (*Smiling: pointing*) Hey ey ey.

JEFF: That's all you are. That's what I thought first

time I saw you. That's what I think now. (*To* ANGELA) Come on. Over here. Walk past him.

JACKO: (*Intercepting* ANGELA *again.*) Daddy Jacko will get round to you later. Daddy Jacko will slap Jeffie's bum.

BAILEY: (*Laughing*) You mad bugger, Jacko. (*To* JUDITH) Don't worry . . .

JUDITH: (*Despite this and* JEFF'*s comments she's wary. It could be a routine between them.*) I just want you lot out of here . . .

(*She looks scared for a minute, trapped, as* BAILEY *steps back to door. But he's only about to call to* JACKO *to go.*)

BAILEY: Come on, Jacko. There's nothing for you, here.

(JACKO *suddenly grabs* ANGELA.)

JACKO: Look at it. In it, lovely?

ANGELA: Oh . . . Oh . . . Christ. Get off!

JUDITH: (*To* BAILEY) Why don't you stop him? You're big enough.

BAILEY: He's only mucking about . . . That's it, Jacko, let's go. Come on, Jeff . . . Let's go . . .

JEFF: Shit! Look at that!

(BAILEY *turns from door to see* JACKO *moving against* ANGELA, *giving her a dry rub, performing his snake dance up against her. He is getting more and more involved. He is not joking. His eyes are glazed.* ANGELA, *whilst this is happening, has her head over* JACKO'*s shoulder, her head back. She is looking away, trying not to look at anyone. There is shame and panic in her eyes. She is trying not to get involved with* JACKO. *She is fighting it, crying out as* JACKO *becomes more forceful in his movements.* BAILEY *gives a sharp laugh, a harsh, stunned laugh.* JEFF *has his mouth open. His expression is beginning to form into pure hatred of what he is seeing.*)

BAILEY: Jacko! You crazy bastard.

(JACKO, *lost now, pushes* ANGELA *back up over the desk. His mouth goes down to her throat. He bites at her, carresses her*

ACT TWO 101

hips. The others watch, hypnotized. Then ANGELA *tears her head right away from* JACKO. *There are tears of anger in her eyes, tears of bewilderment.*

ANGELA: Oh . . . Oh . . . for Christ's sake. Get off me. Please. Get him off me. Somebody. Please. You stink. You stinking pig. You stinking Pi . . . ig.

JACKO: (*Stopping at this.*) Aw, hey, that's not nice . . . Oh no, that's not nice at all . . . is it, Baby . . . ? But this is.

(JACKO *shoves his hand under* ANGELA'S *skirt.*)

JUDITH: (*Suddenly folding her arms across her chest, looking away. Then to* BAILEY:) Stop him . . .

BAILEY: Jacko. I'm off. Stop fooling . . .

JACKO: (*To* ANGELA) Why, you're all wet, darlin'. You want it as bad as me . . .

BAILEY: Jacko . . .

JACKO: Can't leave her like this, Bailey . . . She's sopping for me . . .

ANGELA: No. Please . . .

(JACKO *thrusts* ANGELA *back, unzips himself and pushes himself in between* ANGELA'S *legs.*)

JUDITH: Stop him. Stop him.

JEFF: (*To* BAILEY, *moving toward* JACKO.) Come on, Bailey . . .

(JACKO, *still thrusting at* ANGELA, *trying to stop her wriggling and thrashing on the table, becomes aware of* JEFF *and* BAILEY.)

BAILEY: (*Holding haversack by the sling, ready to swing it with lunch pail inside it.*) Jacko. Silly sod. Give up. Now.

(*He's still expecting that* JACKO *will stop acting the goat and let* ANGELA *up off the table.* ANGELA *is beside herself, crying out.*)

ANGELA: Get him off me. Please. Don't let him do this. To me. I don't want this. I don't want it . . .

JEFF: Bastard Jacko.

JUDITH: (*Recovering approaching* JACKO) Pull him off.

(*She moves to try and help* JEFF.)

(JACKO *lifts his foot backwards and contemptuously backheels* JEFF *in the groin.* JEFF *doubles up.*)

JACKO: Piss off.

(JEFF *falls back against* JUDITH, *holding himself.*)

JEFF: Bloody hell.

JACKO: (*Grinning*) Whatsamarrer with you lot? Why don't you all get it on? Cure all your ills. What's the matter with you? What else is it all about . . . ?

ANGELA: You Shitehawk. (*Taking advantage of* JACKO *looking away from her, she lashes out and knocks* JACKO *back.*)

JACKO: (*Pushes* ANGELA *over table again. Dives on top of her. This time there's no doubt his intentions are serious.*) Right, you bitch. You loverly, loverly bitch, this time you're gonna get yours aren't yer! I'm really gonna screw the arse off you!

BAILEY: Jacko. You'll have us in jail.

(JACKO *is just about getting* ANGELA *in position. All the fight seem to be out of her.*)

JACKO: (*Holding* ANGELA *in position. Ready.*) What's the matter, Bailey? All talk aren't you? A dab hand at card games, eh? Aren't you. No bottle at real games, eh? You thought I was only talking, didn't you? But I'm not, am I? It's you who's all bloody talk. Look at you. There's a bint (JUDITH) screaming for it and you don't do anything. Come on. Get it on. Or hold this one down for me. Come on. Hold the bitch down.

(ANGELA, *just when it looks as if she's given in, bites* JACKO'S *hand and she almost gets free.*)

JACKO: You bitch. You fucking bitch.

(ANGELA *follows this up by lashing out at* JACKO, *hitting him in the face so he's forced to move back.* BAILEY *moves in on*

ACT TWO 103

him, swinging the haversack, but JACKO *ducks and shoulders* BAILEY *in the midriff, knocking him back. He manages to keep* ANGELA *trapped as* JUDITH *goes in to the attack, trying to pull* JACKO *away from* ANGELA.)

JACKO: I'll get round to you. Don't be hasty . . . It ain't your turn yet . . .

(*He belts* JUDITH *off out of it, but by this time* JEFF *has recovered and he lays in on* JACKO. JACKO *holds him off.*)

JACKO: Wassermarrer? Wassermarrer, Sunshine, you want some o' this, eh? Here, look, you want this . . .

(JEFF *stops, looks down on* ANGELA.)

JACKO: It's yours, Man, she's ready . . .

(ANGELA *again makes a move to escape.* JEFF, *after hesitation, jumps on* JACKO. *There is another melee with* JUDITH *also mixed up in it.* JACKO *and* JEFF *lash away at each other. Finally* JEFF *gets in a blow that knocks* JACKO *away from* ANGELA *and toward* BAILEY. JACKO *tries to get back to* ANGELA. BAILEY *hangs on to him and butts him.* ANGELA *free jumps on* JACKO, *hammering at him with her fists.*)

ANGELA: You bastard! You filthy stinking rat-pig, think I'd let you do me, you filthy stinkhole bastard . . .

JACKO: (*Staggering about blindly, his pants round his ankles.*) For Chrissake! For Chrissake! I'm bleeding! Oh my . . . Jesus . . . Mary and . . . Jeeze . . .

BAILEY: (*Stopping* ANGELA. *Holding her.*) That's enough.

JACKO: Oh, me fucking nose. Fucking hell. Me nose. Bailey. It's broke. I can't see. I'm blind . . . Oh, fuckin' hell . . .

(*Blood is streaming down his face, even in his eyes. The t-shirt is torn off him. There are welts on his back where* ANGELA *has hit him.* ANGELA *hits him again.* BAILEY *pushes her off. She is spent. She sobs hysterically, the nerves getting to her.*)

ANGELA: Bastards . . . all bastards . . .

JACKO: Me fuckin' nose is ruined. Bailey, you bastard.

BAILEY: (*Holding* JACKO *still. Wiping his face off with the t-*

shirt he's ripped away from him.) Hold still. You'd have had us in jail. You mad get. I've got a wife and kids. I didn't want this. I didn't want this. (*To* JACKO) Larkin' about's all right, but not this. Shooting the bull is all right, but not this. This ain't right, Man. It's sick. You hurt her. You hurt her bad.

(ANGELA *is held by* JUDITH.)

ANGELA: Filthy stinking pigs, the lot of you.

JUDITH: Okay now . . . Okay . . .

JACKO: Me nose, Bailey. Me poor fucking nose. I'll have you shot, Bailey. I'll have you fucking run over. I'm bleeding to death . . .

BAILEY: Keep your head back, Jacko. It'll be all right.

JACKO: You'd better take to the Ossie. Jeff. Where's Jeff.

JEFF: I'm taking you nowhere, you arsehole.

JACKO: Jeff. Friend.

JEFF: Don't even talk to me.

BAILEY: Come on, Jacko. You'll be all right.

JUDITH: Get him out of here. Look at the mess. This is our work ruined . . . Get him out . . .

ANGELA: (*Screaming.*) Get out you filthy stinking pigs.

JUDITH: All right, Angela. All right, my love. Calm down. No one will hurt you now. Get him out of here.

JACKO: Bastard Bailey. You shouldn't have stopped me. Should have helped me. We could all have had some fun. It's what we all wanted. Didn't need to end up like this. Honest . . . No need. If everybody had been straight. We'd have had fun . . .

BAILEY: Come on, pull your damned pants up, let's go.

JACKO: Oh . . . oh . . . Oh . . . you're all talk Bailey . . .

BAILEY: And you're sick.

JACKO: I'll spread the word on you, Bailey.

ACT TWO 105

BAILEY: (*Leading* JACKO *through door to stairs.*) Just keep your head back. (*To* JUDITH.) Don't say anything about this, will you?

JUDITH: Get out of here.

BAILEY: (*Harder.*) I'm warning you.

JUDITH: Get out.

(BAILEY *exits with* JACKO.)

ANGELA: (*Recovering, bit by bit*) Filthy rotten sod . . .

JUDITH: You gave him a few bruises to remember you by.

ANGELA: Yes. I did. Didn't I? He'd have got more too if that other ape hadn't pulled me back. I'da slaughtered him. Filthy stinking pig. He stank like a midden. Think I'd want him. And all because I was having a bit of a joke with them . . .

JUDITH: Yes . . . (*A glance at* JEFF) Well . . .

ANGELA: God they made me feel sick . . . And look at me.

JUDITH: You'll be all right. Sit down a while. Take it easy.

ANGELA: Don't tell Frank will you?

JUDITH: Don't you think you should?

ANGELA: No. For God's sake. Not Frank. Christ. I feel filthy. I'll kill that bastard Jacko if I see him again. I'll do him . . . Oh, has he marked me. On my neck? (*Love bite*)

JUDITH: It's not much.

ANGELA: Does it show?

JUDITH: Not much.

ANGELA: Frank'll go mad. Why did this have to happen? Couldn't they see I was only having them on?

JUDITH: Here, borrow this neckerchief.

ANGELA: Thanks.

JUDITH: Comb your hair down this side.

ANGELA: Do I look all right?

JUDITH: Yes. You're fine.

ANGELA: Sure.

JUDITH: Yes.

JEFF: Listen. I have to say. I'm very sorry for what happened here . . .

ANGELA: (*Swinging round*) What's he doing here? You still here, stinkpig?

JEFF: Look. I'm sorry. It wasn't me.

ANGELA: Why didn't you clear off with those other bastards?

JEFF: I just wanted to make sure you were all right. I wanted to say I was sorry. I suppose, really, it was my fault. I know I shouldn't have brought them across here. I . . . I . . . well, I shouldn't that's all. That Jacko. I didn't want to have anything to do with what happened here.

ANGELA: You did though, didn't you . . . ?

JEFF: No. I tried to stop it. (*To* JUDITH) Didn't I?

ANGELA: You just didn't have the guts that's all.

JEFF: No. You've got me wrong.

ANGELA: You're just the same as they are. You're all the same.

JEFF: No. I wouldn't want it like that. Not me. I'd want it different . . .

ANGELA: Ah, go away. You were with them this afternoon. I saw you down there earlier on. Down there.

JEFF: But it was different then.

ANGELA: You came here because you wanted to . . . you wanted to do what he did . . .

JEFF: No. I came here. Because you waved . . . I . . . thought . . .

ACT TWO

ANGELA: You'd have done it, you just didn't have the guts . . .

JEFF: It's no use talking about it if . . .

(*Sound of car approaching. Sound of car horn. Imperious commanding.*)

ANGELA: (*Panicking*) That'll be Frank. Christ, if he sees me like this. He's such a jealous . . .

JUDITH: Take it easy.

ANGELA: Do I look all right? Oh, there's a button off.

JUDITH: Take this pin. There. You look all right.

ANGELA: Sure? I'd better go down. If he comes up here and sees this mess. And him still here, he'll . . .

(*Car horn again. Louder. More commanding.*)

(ANGELA *is suddenly stung by this.*)

ANGELA: Bloody hell.

JUDITH: Better go.

ANGELA: Rudolph Bloody 'Itler, I don't need this. (*Horn again*) All right. I'm coming. Keep yer bloody hair on . . .

JUDITH: Cheerio . . .

ANGELA: If he starts I'll . . . I'm ready for him . . . Oh, I'm sorry . . . Cheerio . . . I'll see you . . .

JUDITH: Yes. I'll see you.

ANGELA: Right, you make sure (*She leaves as car horn sounds again.*) All right. I'm coming. Sounding yer horn at me. Yer'll get yer bloody answer . . .

(*Exit* ANGELA.)

(JUDITH *begins to tidy up.* JEFF *begins to help her. They pause, maybe to hear shouting going on off. Car doors slamming. Car purring away out of the lot.*)

JEFF: I should have known better. Should have known that Jacko was really a psycho. But I really didn't believe he'd go that far. I'd never seen anything like this before, just thought it was all just a lot of men talk. I didn't think with me and Bailey with him he'd do anything. Just thought he'd mess around. But you know, he meant it. He'd have done it. And for a minute or two there I thought she wanted it too. I thought she was going to let him. You know, I think if she'd been on her own. She would. If you hadn't been here she'd have . . . Maybe, I'm wrong. I don't know. I mean Jesus. That Jacko. And that Bailey. That's what I have to put up with all day over at work. I don't know. Sometimes I think they're all right. Just funny. I mean they can't help it. I mean they don't need it. They can be okay. They've got a lot in them. Jacko, he could turn his hand to anything. He's brighter than he thinks. He's brighter than me, really, but then he just flips. Same with Bailey. He can be a good guy. Quite like him. But then they come on like this. I'm not putting up with it any more. I've had enough of it. That's one thing. I'm not wasting my life, so I end up like Bailey and Jacko. No way. I'm getting out while I'm still young enough too. Look at me though, I'm shaking . . . Still shaking. She got over it faster'n me.

JUDITH: (*Having finished tidying up.*) Want a cigarette? (*She produces packet from her bag.*)

JEFF: No. Ta. I don't.

(JUDITH *puts cigarette between her lips.*)

JEFF: But, yes, go on. I will.

(*He takes cig she has lit with trembling fingers, puts it uncertainly between his lips. Making pig's arse of the end paper,* JUDITH *lights another cigarette for herself.*)

JEFF: (*Going over to window, inhaling cigarette.*) She was a silly bitch that one.

JUDITH: No. Not really. She was an innocent. She's got a dad who treats her like a princess. She's been able to trust up to now. She thinks she can say anything and do anything and get away with it. Never needed to think. Now it's owning up time. Now she's got to start thinking for herself. It isn't going to be easy for her.

ACT TWO

JEFF: I thought she was going to let him.

JUDITH: It's over with now. Why are you dwelling on it?

JEFF: Can't get the picture out of my head. For one minute there. I . . . I thought I was in a mad house. I . . . Turned me up it did to see it. Wasn't funny.

JUDITH: Why did you come with them?

JEFF: I was conned into giving them a lift.

JUDITH: Oh, I see. Conned, were you?

JEFF: Honest. No kidding. I . . . Well . . . I . . . Look, don't get me wrong. I wanted to come. Ye'. I mean. I was curious. But I wouldn't have. Don't think I'd have. Don't put me with Jacko. Not me . . .

JUDITH: Mmmm. (JUDITH *continues looking over at* JEFF, *until he shuffles embarrassedly.*) No, you're different. You've got more in you, have you?

JEFF: (*Picking up her sarcasm. Stung into answering straight and firmly.*) Yes. Now. Up to today, I don't know. After today. Yes. I have . . .

JUDITH: It's okay. It's okay . . .

JEFF: But I am owning up. It was my fault. They wouldn't have seen her or you if I hadn't pointed her out to them. They didn't see her at first. I was the only one who knew you were here. But they were buggering me about, especially Jacko. I couldn't put up with any more of it. I just used you as a diversion. It was weak of me. It wouldn't happen again. But I didn't think Jacko would . . .

JUDITH: It's over now.

JEFF: Yes.

(JUDITH *takes out comb. Combs her hair.* JEFF *watches her.*)

JEFF: But I'm still sorry.

JUDITH: Look. Forget it. It's all over. You're absolved.

JEFF: Thank you.

JUDITH: I want to lock up now.

JEFF: Oh. Right. (*But he doesn't move.*)

JUDITH: (*With her bag and the key, etc.*) So, if you're ready ...

JEFF: Oh. Right. (*He shuffles around and then finally says:*) Look. Would you like a lift somewhere? If you want. Which way are you going? I've got a car. Well, it's an old banger but it goes and I could. I would. I mean. Don't get me wrong. I'm not pushing. It's up to you. But, I mean, if you wanted after I've dropped you off I could come back when you're ready and we could go out for a trip. I know this spot up in the hills. Nobody goes there. It hasn't been spoiled yet. There's a wood. Pine. Silent like a cathedral. There's this pond. A big lake. You can sit up on the rocks and watch the sun go down over it. So peaceful up there and clean. Fresh. Like a new world. You could begin to believe in something up there. I mean, don't misunderstand me. I'd hate for you to misunderstand me. I ... We could take my dog. You like dogs? I got a dog. She's lovely. Short-haired German Pointer. She loves it up there. That's if you want. I'm not pushing myself on you ... Er ... What do you er ... think?

JUDITH: Why not?

JEFF: Eh? Yes?

JUDITH: Yes. All right. Come on then. You're on.

JEFF: Jesus. No kidding?

JUDITH: Let's go.

JEFF: Wow.

(*She moves to door.* JEFF, *relieved, smiling, happy like a kid, follows her. She lets him out. Looks back into the office. Breathes deeply, wryly, slowly, then follows after* JEFF, *closing and locking the door behind her.*)

(*Lights: The silence of the office. The evening sun's rays slanting in. The piles of finished invoices.*)

Act Two

(*The lights fade slowly down and out with sound of* JEFF *revving up his car off.*)

(*The exhaust is faulty so it sounds crackly, loud, and sort of powerful, like a racing car.*)

(*End of play*)

Prop List

Stage One: "Office"
Table
Two chairs
Adding machines
Pens and pencils
Batches of invoices
Sandwiches
Cigarettes
Sweets (candies)
Chewing gum

Stage Two: "River Bank"
Packing case
Pieces of driftwood
Flagon of ale (bottle of beer)
JACKO's mouth organ
JEFF's book
Sticks

tes:

The "window" in the Office is only suggested; there is viously no actual window.

When it states in the script that the men and the women k at each other across the river, they don't actually look ach other across the stage; rather, they look out into the lience. They do *not* make eye contact.

or final scene—river bank material is cleared; both stages ome as one.